THE SOUL
OF MODERN
ECONOMIC
MAN

THE SOUL
OF MODERN
ECONOMIC
MAN

Ideas of Self-Interest

THOMAS HOBBES TO
ADAM SMITH

Milton L. Myers

THE UNIVERSITY OF CHICAGO PRESS
Chicago and London

Milton L. Myers has published several journal articles on the history of economic thought of the seventeenth and eighteenth centuries. His current research focuses on the pre-Marxian critics of industrialism.

THE UNIVERSITY OF CHICAGO PRESS, CHICAGO 60637
THE UNIVERSITY OF CHICAGO PRESS, LTD., LONDON

Library of Congress Cataloging in Publication Data

Myers, Milton L. (Milton Linwood), 1926-
    The soul of modern economic man.

    Includes bibliographical references and index.
    1. Economics—Moral and ethical aspects—History.
2. Self-interest—History. I. Title. II. Title:
Economic man.
HB72.M82 1983   330   82-23790
ISBN 0-226-55448-1

No science can be more secure than the unconscious
metaphysics which tacitly it presupposes.
                              Alfred North Whitehead

Contents

Contents

Preface

This work is an outgrowth of an encounter in the stacks of the Yale University Library with the writings of certain eighteenth-century British moral philosophers. I had been searching for early works on the division of labor by writers on business and economic subjects who are mentioned in the standard texts on the history of economic thought. But, somehow, the trail led toward writers who are seldom, if ever, mentioned in these texts. I found that these moral philosophers on the division of labor were not interested in the usual economic aspects of the principle, as, for example, profit and the balance of trade, but rather in the social effects of the principle, its power to pull people into social relationships and to keep them there. These philosophers were any thing but writers on business and economic topics and yet they were vitally concerned with a basic economic principle in what I felt to be a different and important way. Further searching among these writers led me to believe that there is more to eighteenth-century economic ideas than what is covered in the textbooks. It is out of these explorations that this book developed.

After the first draft of this book was largely completed, I came across Albert O. Hirschman's *The Passions and the Interests* (Princeton, N.J.: Princeton University Press, 1977). I saw immediately that Hirschman and I had been working along similar lines of thought but with very different viewpoints, his being largely political and mine essentially economic. Any reader interested in other aspects of the idea of self-interest in the eighteenth century would do well to read *The Passions and the Interests*.

I wish to acknowledge the aid of a number of people who helped bring this book to completion. Janet Swift obtained obscure works from remote libraries to speed my research. Tom Dulack gave general suggestions and encouragement as the book was being written. Royall Brandis, Warren Samuels, and Joseph Cropsey offered detailed criticism which, I hope, has led to improvements in the book.

Leonard Peters originally suggested my writing this work and, trustingly, offered to read my first tentative efforts on the subject. This led to a considerable effort on his part. I wish to thank him, especially, for the interested and generous spirit he offered to this work.

1
Introduction

John Maynard Keynes once commented about the influence of ideas on men of politics and affairs. In concluding remarks at the end of his great work, *The General Theory of Employment, Interest, and Money* (1936), he said, "Practical men, who believe themselves to be exempt from any intellectual influences, are usually the slaves of some defunct economist." Keynes wrote this trenchant remark after he had been working for a decade or more to throw off the controlling influence of classical economics from British economic policy. The British economy had stagnated during the 1920s, and a general depression had settled on the world in the following decade. The laissez-faire attitudes of the British and most other governments in the face of this economic crisis appalled Keynes. Government intervention to revive these economies was necessary. He was struggling to establish the point that free-market economies cannot be expected to maintain full employment and prosperity at all times, that such economies can slump into lengthy depressions and, indeed, can remain depressed for very protracted periods of time. Men of power who believed otherwise were being deluded by the quietist recommendations of classical economics. To Keynes, faith in the natural resilience of economies motivated by self-interest was an idea whose time had passed. The belief that, given time, a depressed free-market economy would always rebound to prosperity was, to Keynes, based on erroneous economics, not to mention wishful thinking. In short he argued that self-interest did not under all circumstances promote the public welfare. Keynes sardonically reminded those who had been patiently waiting for years for the curative power of private enterprise to reassert itself that, also, "In the long run we are all dead."

Keynes's comments about the influence of classical economics raises an important question. If the classical economist influenced men of power and shaped the mistaken policies of state, might one not ask: Who, originally, shaped the values of the classical economist? If Keynes's "defunct economist" is to be charged with influencing the decisions of state, who in turn is to be charged with influencing the ideas of the classical economist? The present book will attempt to answer that question.

Before proceeding I should clarify what I mean by the influencing and shaping of the ideas of the classical economist. I am not referring to the long development of the technical apparatus of classical economics, to the evolution of the finely wrought logic of supply and demand in a free-market system. And I am not concerned with the refining and perfecting of the mathematical language, so important for the expression of the ideas of the classical economist. I am looking for something more fundamental. I am searching for those influences which gave birth to the body of classical economics in the first place. This is not a matter of studying the development of the contents of classical economics, but rather a question of those influences which, originally, caused the whole subject to come into being toward the end of the eighteenth century.

We will see that classical economics came into being as an answer to a problem which had been challenging some of the best minds in moral philosophy for almost a century before Adam Smith. This classic problem dealt with the relationship between self-interest and the public welfare. We will find that classical economics was a product of this problem, as it was intensively investigated by the philosophical predecessors of Adam Smith. I am going to describe these investigations which so occupied Smith's predecessors, to show how self-interest, which I will call the soul of modern economic man, gradually developed into an acceptable and, eventually, into a highly commended drive for modern man. These philosophers and theologians, who were anticipating laissez-faire, were also creating and ratifying an economic soul of self-interest for modern man.

Who were these minds anticipating laissez-faire? Who were these writers calling classical economics into being? Their personal lives and daily interests varied greatly. They were not a school; they did not think, work, or live together. Most were decided individualists as they studied the individual. Some were clergymen serving country parishes who wrote books, often very long, tedious, and involved, on the nature of man as they attempted to justify his earthly ways in the higher processes of creation. Some were men of letters translating current opinions about the nature of man and society into popular books and essays or, in a few cases, into poetry. A few were men of affairs who moved in important political and social circles but who, nevertheless, were intrigued by the study of the deeper foundations of social life. And a few we might call academics because of their attachment to universities. Their interests lay largely in the writing of learned treatises in moral philosophy. Some were famous in their own time, quite a few were obscure then as they are now. Some were well-connected and well-to-do, a few were not. Some came from the most conservative of backgrounds, a few were radicals. But all these writers, with their diverse backgrounds, had a passionate interest in understanding the basic character of man and society, which they felt must be placed in the larger context of the processes of nature and of all creation. To them, man and society could not be properly understood and fully appreciated unless studied as part of this larger context. They were students of nature in the largest possible sense. They saw man, either individually or collectively, as part of a higher work. This was the basic premise underlying their writings.

From this belief in the overriding importance of nature they derived the principle of design, an idea crucial to the reasonings of just about all of them. The principle of design is based on the belief that all causes lead to ordered effects. If the world, and all within it, operates in a precise and dependable pattern (and they believed there was abundant evidence that it did), then man acting as an individual and as a social being must be subject to this immanent and all-pervading order. Man is a product of the operations of nature, so he can be understood only in terms of the patterns of nature. These patterns can be analyzed and understood and, as a result, so can man. Understanding the design in nature leads to an understanding of the design in man.

Arthur Lovejoy, that very great mind in the history of ideas, said that each age is dominated by a set of "implicit or incompletely explicit *assumptions*, or more or less *unconscious mental habits*" which predisposes it "to think in terms of certain categories or of particular types of imagery."[1] These are "endemic assumptions" controlling "the course of man's reflections on almost any subject,"[2] and Lovejoy called such a pervasive thought a "unit idea."[3] As our writers stood on the earth, looking upward at the immensity of the heavens and downward at the incredible detail of plants and animals, they felt deeply the design in all creation. The principle of design became their unit idea, and it had a critical influence in shaping their interpretations of man and society. Their arguments conclude that self-interest serves the ends of society, and how they arrived at this conclusion greatly depends on the principle of design.

These philosophical anticipators of laissez-faire were spurred to their work on self-interest by the stand taken by Thomas Hobbes. During the middle of the seventeenth century Hobbes published several works, the most prominent being his famous *Leviathan* (1651). In this work he identified self-interest as the most powerful drive in man. He argued that this drive knew no bounds and that it pushes man into the greatest of excesses as he strives to satisfy it. As a result, a life in society is impossible. The only way that man can overcome an existence full of aggressiveness and destruction is to submit his powers to an absolute authority. Authoritarian government is an absolute necessity if man wishes to live in peace and enjoy the obvious benefits of a life in society. Our writers will spend the century following Hobbes rebutting his harsh indictment of man and, especially, his interpretation of man as a being driven by a self-interest that is insatiable and destructive.

The methods they will use to answer Hobbes fall into three categories. The earliest opponents of Hobbes call upon principles of psychology to answer his indictment of self-interest. They say that man's mind is composed of various motives, self-interest being just one of a number. They then argue that there exists in the mind a natural balance among all of these motives, and that this balance tends to keep each motive, including self-interest, within certain bounds. The result is a moderated self-interest, whose results in society are constructive, not destructive. The next group of opponents of Hobbes feel it necessary to place their arguments on a firmer foundation, for they feel that the evanescent and changing nature of the feelings hidden within the mind will not do. So they are drawn toward harder and more precise principles, those of physics, especially the newly discovered laws of Newtonian physics. They interpret the drive of self-interest in man as the moral equivalent of the force of gravity in nature, as they argue that both self-interest and gravity are similar because each tends to draw all things toward a certain point. Just as gravitation produces a coordinated movement among the planetary bodies, so self-interest acts to organize constructively the movements of human bodies in society. Again, self-interest is made to serve the ends of society.

Both the psychological and physical arguments saw self-interest serving the public welfare, and each had its strong supporters, but such arguments were not preferred by our next group of writers. This group desired to prove the social efficacy of self-interest on the basis of something more common, visible, and mundane than either the principles of psychology or physics. They struck upon the division of labor as an answer. Here was a principle existing everywhere, one found among all of the common procedures of making a living. These writers saw that individuals naturally differ in their skills, aptitudes, and interests. It seemed to them only natural for the individual to capitalize on these differences, to pursue that kind of work best suited to the skills that made him different from other workers; in short, to pursue his own self-interest. As the individual does so, he himself will benefit by being more productive, and society will also benefit from a higher collective productivity. Trade will, necessarily, have to follow in order to distribute the surpluses of each worker throughout society to the benefit of all. Although the end result will be self-interest serving the public welfare, the members of this group saw their argument toward this end resting on a

4

much firmer foundation than the previous ones that depended on a balance of motives in the mind or on moral gravitation. This last group of writers is moving in the direction of an economic solution to the problem of self-interest and the public welfare but, as we will see, they were in no sense economists, at least as economists are categorized today.

Finally, I come to my last writer, Adam Smith. The present book will attempt to show that Smith's economics takes shape as an answer to the same problem facing these previous writers. Smith devises what we would call a genuinely economic solution to the classic problem of self-interest and the public welfare, and I will analyze the reasons why he chose this kind of solution. I will present Smith as the last, most effective, and, surely, most influential of a long line of writers who were replying to Hobbes's interpretation of self-interest.

Philosophy might be described as a changing residue of uncategorized and unanswered questions which have preoccupied leading minds throughout the ages. In this period before Smith, the problem of the social implications of self-interest was a leading, if not the dominant, unanswered question plaguing the minds in British moral philosophy. It provided a recurring theme in the writings of many of the leading minds of the period. Once in a great while a seminal mind appears, approaches the tangle of questions that is philosophy, teases out of the tangle a seemingly intractable problem, then applies new or revolutionary insights to it, and, in so doing, creates a new science. A science is a product of its problem. The problem giving birth to the science of political economy was how to resolve the drive of self-interest in terms of the social welfare. It is Adam Smith who teases this problem out of British moral philosophy, applies a radically new method to solving it, and gives us the beginnings of a new science, political economy. Out of these beginnings evolved classical economics.

I plan to use categories common to the eighteenth-century mind in our analysis of one of the leading ideas of that century. I do not believe that twentieth-century values and attitudes will get us very far in appreciating and understanding an eighteenth-century idea. Current categories of thought miss much of crucial importance for understanding the intellectual development of the idea of self-interest during the eighteenth century. Very little of what I will be doing here is discussed in the standard histories of economic thought, because these histories define their subject in the terms that are current today. These books will do if one is interested in the content of economics itself. But they will not serve very well if one is interested in how economics emerged as an answer to a much-discussed question in moral philosophy. They look back at economics from the viewpoint of this century. In contrast, I will be looking forward toward what will become economics. This view is from an entirely different set of standards, those of eighteenth-century moral philosophers, a group that could not have conceived of the twentieth century, not to mention the categories of the twentieth-century economists.

Current economists pride themselves on the "hard" nature of their science. Dealing with the realities of wealth and resources, gross national products and levels of employment, they evoke in themselves feelings of the practical, the useful, the concrete. Compared to other social sciences, they enjoy a subject lending itself to rigorous quantification, which reinforces their feelings for the relevance of their subject. While a few of our eighteenth-century moral philosophers attempted to measure some of the things they dealt with, they were, indeed, not nearly so quantity-oriented in their thinking as many are today. Their primary concern was the quality of life, and they felt that this depended on the inner character of the individual. They were not so much concerned with earthly institutions and materials controlling the life of man as with the higher laws of nature controlling man and everything else in the universe. Current economists will not feel at home with this type of mind. Yet, it was this type of thinking which stimulated other minds to start to think in economic terms.

Jacob Viner, one of the rare twentieth-century economic minds capable of ranging beyond things merely economic, was aware that modern economics grew out of something more than only the work of economists. In his classic *Studies in the Theory of International Trade* (1937), he wrote, "The antecedents of Smith's laissez-faire and free trade views are probably rightly to be sought mainly in the philosophic literature . . . rather than in the earlier English economic literature."[4] He repeated this point later in a paper entitled "The Intellectual History of Laissez-Faire" (1959), in which he argued that "In England the most important developments which finally prepared the ground for the formulation of an economic doctrine of laissez-faire consisted of the contributions of moral philosophers and theologians whose major objective was often to rebut Hobbes."[5] Viner was conscious that certain categories of ideas, unseemly to current economists, were quite influential in shaping the beginnings of their subject. Unfortunately, all we have from Viner on this question are a few scattered comments and one short paper. Today, with the revival of interest in free-market economics it would seem appropriate, even important, to try to gain a deeper understanding of what made classical economics come about, to try to understand how the subject got to be the way it did. Viner has pointed the direction in which to explore for an answer. The present book will take that direction. It will examine in greater detail the ground that Viner pointed to but did not find time to explore sufficiently.

6

It is one thing to trace the intellectual history of an idea; it is quite another to find how that idea came to be a widely accepted value in society. Tracing an idea is not the same thing as explaining how the idea became a common standard of social conduct. I will, however, attempt to do both. The idea that self-interest could serve the public welfare was worked out in considerable detail by our moral philosophers and theologians long before any organized group of political economists came to the same conclusion but in different terms. The political economists disseminated in their own terms an idea already discovered and cultivated by our arbiters of social values. It is doubtful if they could have done this if these earlier arbiters had not cleared the way for them. As R. H. Tawney noted, the standards which provide the foundation for general approval of a type of social conduct are primarily moral and intellectual.[6] It was by establishing such standards that our arbiters of social values enabled the economic theories of the classical economists to find wide support later on.

I

THE PROBLEM POSED

2
The Soul of Modern Economic Man

We are in search of the essential and animating principle in the character of modern economic man. We are looking for the inner drive dominating all of his other motives. Our period begins with the commercial revolution and ends with the coming of large-scale industrialism. Our setting is Britain because economic man thrived there as nowhere else during this time. At the beginning of this period the growth of British foreign trade exceeded that of any other nation and, later, Britain led the world into the industrial revolution. Adam Smith looked askance at the practices and policies of British businessmen, calling Britain a "nation of shopkeepers," but he also was fully aware that Britain was the home of the great admirals of commerce. And, in the following century, when Thomas Carlyle was denigrating his "Captains of Industry," he also recognized their leadership in the world. Britain is the place to look for the soul of modern economic man.

To gain deeper insights into the character of economic man I will examine the works of a number of writers who have discussed the kind of life this man leads and the things he does. We want comments from a diversity of viewpoints and backgrounds, from the scholarly to the popular, from the philosophical to the literary, including the views of essayists, novelists, and poets. We do not want one point of view, we want many. This will help give us a balanced estimation of the character of economic man. Sometimes these treatments of him will be favorable, other times very unfavorable. They will range from admiration, occasionally verging on adulation, all the way to the most bitter attacks on his character and his works. In looking over this diversity of opinions and viewpoints, we hope to discover some common denominator underlying the character of economic man. We will find this common denominator to be self-interest. This is the soul of modern economic man.

I begin with the Puritans. They are a point of controversy among writers on historical subjects and much has been written for and against them.

11

But I will confine my attention to those three classic works concerning Puritanism and, more generally, the influence of Protestantism on modern economic values and attitudes: Max Weber, *The Protestant Ethic and the Spirit of Capitalism* (1904–5), Ernst Troeltsch, *Protestantism and Progress* (1902, English trans.), and R. H. Tawney, *Religion and the Rise of Capitalism* (1926).

The foundation of Puritan beliefs is a strong feeling of the importance of the individual in the divine plan. This is a result of an intense feeling of a one-to-one relationship with God. The Puritan requires few external aids to help him in his very personal confrontation with God. There is little need for earthly institutions and formalisms to mediate his relationship with the divine. Consequently, much of the material paraphernalia of other religious groups is rejected by the Puritan. He stands alone as he seeks salvation and cannot look to comforting objects and ceremonies in his struggles to save his soul. Every thought, every action in his everyday life is under direct scrutiny from above. There is nothing standing between him and God. He cannot employ any interest group to plead his cause with God.

This intense consciousness of the divine demands great seriousness toward the daily routines of life. Occasional good works in order to save one's soul are not enough. Salvation is a full-time job. The Puritan must devote all his waking hours to the salvation of his soul because he has to strive alone. No person or institution can help him as he faces the awful immensity of eternity by himself. Such fervent feelings would force some individuals into a monastery, into a life of religious asceticism. But the Puritan, due to his active nature, chooses, instead, a worldly asceticism to help himself reduce his religious anxiety. Any ascetic leads a life of rigorous self-discipline, and labor has been one of the accepted ascetic techniques. The famed Puritan work ethic follows from this. Labor provides the means in ordinary life to save one's soul.

But the results of constant work create a problem. Continual dedication to work leads to the accumulation of wealth, and how can worldly goods be the proper fruit of genuine religious inspiration? Is not material prosperity an indication of spiritual poverty? The Puritan mind resolved this problem by relegating the material gains from work to a lesser category, that of a mere by-product of the higher spiritual struggle. Material gains were not seen as the end products of spiritual worthiness but only as transient stuff thrown off in the never-ending struggle for salvation. What is important is the intensity of the mental and physical involvement of the individual in his work, not the material results of the work. The goods that happen to be accumulated may be looked upon as external signs of the intense spiritual effort their owner underwent. This, in itself, justifies the existence of the goods.

If intense work is a feature of the character of modern economic man, then Puritan attitudes must be given some credit for infusing this ethic into his soul. But the Puritan sees strenuous business activity only as a means to save one's soul, and this is a very narrow and constricted view of work. Work is utterly personal, its purpose begins and ends with the soul of the individual. Clearly, this feeling of the utter inwardness of work has not been as prominent since Puritan times. So, while we can see the Puritan helping to instill the value of work into the soul of modern economic man, we can hardly give him credit for the later view that the personal economic effort and decision of the individual can be justified because it is seen to serve the public welfare. The single-mindedness of the Puritan viewpoint does not encompass the idea that efforts at self-interest serve the public welfare. Spiritual feelings seldom extend into external concerns about society.

As we move into the eighteenth century we begin to perceive a changing attitude toward work, a growing interest in its social, as opposed to its personal, implications. Attitudes toward economic man open up as writers begin to realize that the activities of the businessman that he carries on entirely for his own personal gain have, nevertheless, far wider implications for the group and even the entire nation. Eventually, some writers will go so far as to surmise that individual economic effort is, at base, the foundation for the arts and, even, the advance of civilization.[1] Self-interest is made to serve not only the general welfare but even the muses. Prominent and less prominent figures from the world of literature will now begin to extol the virtues of the merchant, manufacturer, and trader. If the Enlightenment is the great period for liberal and generous attitudes toward the arts and sciences, it is no less so for attitudes toward economic man.

This very positive interest in the world of business and businessmen can be seen early in the eighteenth century in that entertaining but somewhat preachy periodical reflecting middle-class values, *The Spectator* (1711–14). Written largely by Joseph Addison and Richard Steele, the essays in *The Spectator* comment on a wide range of contemporary topics and interests; several of the essays are about trade. The plan for *The Spectator* is to construct these essays around several members of a club, one of whose members is Sir Andrew Freeport, introduced as a "Merchant of great Eminence in the City of *London*." Steele goes on to describe him as a "Person of indefatigable Industry, strong Reason, and great Experience. His Notions of Trade are noble and generous, and . . . he calls the Sea the *British Common*." Steele continually shows his admiration for this man of trade. "A General Trader of good Sense, is pleasanter company than a general Scholar . . . the Perspicuity of his Discourse gives the same Pleasure that Wit would in another Man."[2] In another essay Addison compliments his "worthy Friend Sir ANDREW FREEPORT, a Man of so much natural Eloquence, good Sense, and Probity of Mind, that I always hear him with a particular Pleasure."[3] Economic man has come a long way from the intense and inward-looking Puritan.

Addison and Steele's identification with this man of trade is expressed clearly as they allow Freeport to best Sir Roger De Coverly in an argument over the merits of trade and traders. De Coverly is a fine-humored, well-connected country gentleman who is generous toward his servants and tenants and who enjoys the pleasures of both town and country. But De Coverly looks upon traders as not quite respectable, criticizing them for trimming means to fit their ends. He says, "as Gain is the chief End of such a People, they never pursue any other: The Means to it are never regarded; they will, if it comes easily, get Money honestly; but if not, they will not scruple to attain it by Fraud and Cosenage." He then caps his criticism with the curt comment, "what can there great and noble be expected from him whose Attention is for ever fixed upon ballancing his Books, and watching over his Expenses?"[4] The side that Steele takes in this argument is Freeport's; he gives him more space to reply than he gives to De Coverly and he makes Freeport's replies more pointed and convincing than De Coverly's vague, general criticisms of a stereotype. Freeport reminds De Coverly of the "great and noble Monuments of Charity and publick Spirit which have been erected by Merchants." By "Parsimony and Frugality," by keeping "an Accompt or measure [of] things by the most infallible Way," the merchant is able to afford more work to more artificers than the country gentleman can afford through his hospitality to the countryside. "I believe," Freeport says, "the Families of the Artificers will thank me, more than the Households of the Peasants shall Sir Roger."[5] (De Coverly not only employs his tenants but greatly enjoys giving them rustic entertainments.)

Freeport then compares the daily activities of the merchant with those of the country gentleman. The trader works at finding markets, getting together cargoes, arranging for their transport; he then assumes the risks of all these operations. Freeport asks, "What has the Merchant done that he should be so little in the good Graces of Sir Roger? he throws down on Man's Enclosures, and tramples upon no Man's Corn . . . he pays the poor Man for his Work; he communicates his Profit with Mankind . . . he furnishes Employment and Subsistence to greater Numbers than the richest Nobleman."[6] Finally, Freeport refers to the decline of old landed families caused by the mismanagement of their estates, and how these families have had to "make Way for such new Masters as have been more exact in their Accompts than themselves." And he adds, "certainly he deserves the Estate a great deal better who has got it by his industry, than

The Soul of Modern Economic Man

he who has lost it by his Negligence."[7] This is the end of the argument. Steele does not give De Coverly a chance to reply. Virtue rests more with the merchant and trader than with the country gentleman. Steele, being the gentleman he is, does not seem to be conscious of the motive underlying Freeport's energy and industry, which is, of course, self-interest. But, in any event, Freeport's work is justified because of its superior benefits to society.

The high opinion expressed in *The Spectator* toward trade is repeated in Addison's description of the one place "in the Town which I so much love to frequent," the Royal Exchange. He is impressed by all kinds of traders consulting together—those from the country, from the city, from all parts of the world. He extols the cosmopolitan atmosphere of the Exchange: "Factors in the Trading World are what Ambassadors are in the Politick World; they negociate Affairs, conclude Treaties. . . . I am infinitely delighted in mixing with these several Ministers of Commerce."[8] Addison's emotions expand as he says, "This grand Scene of Business gives me an infinite Variety of solid and substantial Entertainments." His "Heart naturally overflows with Pleasure at the sight of a prosperous and happy Multitude" as he looks upon "such a Body of Men thriving in their own private Fortunes, and at the same time promoting the Publick Stock."[9] He is then carried away by thoughts of the remote and romantic places connected together by trade and of the wonderful and exotic products afforded Britain by this trade. "For these Reasons there are not more useful Members in a Commonwealth than Merchants. They knit Mankind together in a mutual Intercourse of good Offices, distribute the Gifts of Nature, find Work for the Poor, add Wealth to the Rich, and Magnificence to the Great."[10] All of these great and public effects are due to trade, and to traders.

Daniel Defoe, one of the most prolific of English writers, follows Addison and Steele in these generous and expansive sentiments toward trade. In his *A Plan of the English Commerce* (1728) Defoe again takes up the argument about the relative merits of the country gentleman and the man of trade. Again, and even more definitely this time, the man of trade comes out ahead of the country gentleman.

Defoe repeats some of the points which came up in the debate between Freeport and De Coverly, and adds some new ones of his own. Men of trade, it is claimed by their critics, have little dignity and no established station in life. They are really little better than "Mechanicks." Defoe, in order to get to the bottom of this "Jargon" about positions and connections in life, gives a short history of the world so as to point out the very great importance of this supposedly low race of "Mechanicks" to the development of civilization. He claims that Adam's descendants were

15

tinkerers and craftsmen, and that the builders of the Tower of Babel were, obviously, men who worked with their hands. Such workers were held in high esteem by the ancients.[11] If workers were formerly looked upon so favorably, "why then are we to despise Commerce as a Mechanism, and the Trading World as mean . . . ?"[12] Moreover, where would the gentleman be without the trader? He could not dispose of the produce of his countryside without the trader, nor collect the rents on his estate. Without the trader he would be forced to lower himself into trade in order to survive. As *The Spectator* did, Defoe notes the economic decline of noble families while "Mechanicks" rise to refill their ranks in the upper classes.[13] Defoe conducts his attack on the gentry with cutting emphasis as he defends economic man from the pretentious claims of his supposed superiors.

Defoe is aware that the man of business is fully able to stand on his own record. It is not necessary for him to reply to his opponents in order to establish his position in society. Trade is good for the soul, and that is enough. As "the Industry of Mankind is set on Work, their Hopes and Views are rais'd, and their Ambition fir'd: The View and Prospect of Gain inspires the World with the keenest Vigor, puts new Life into their Souls." In contrast, people without trade are "sad and dejected, poor and disconsolate, heavy and indolent . . . for Want of something to labour profitably at."[14] "Employment is Life, Sloth and Indolence is Death; to be busy, is to be chearful, to be pleasant."[15] To emphasize the importance of trade, Defoe likens it to the mother of two daughters, the names of whom he sets out from his text in capital letters, "MANUFACTURE AND NAVIGATION." Their "fruitful Progeny in Arts may be said to employ Mankind. . . . See how they unite their Powers to do good to the World, and to teach Men how to live happy and comfortably."[16] Concluding his comparison of the placid and perhaps stagnant life of the landed gentleman with the active one of the trader, Defoe says, "*an Estate is* but *a Pond*, but *Trade is a Spring*."[17]

But such high praise for the man of business is not confined to Addison, Steele, and Defoe, minds who are interested in the practical side of life and who, appropriately enough, are beginning to express their utilitarian thoughts in the more practical and prosaic forms of modern English. Minds concerned with higher things also show an admiration for trade and traders, as with Edward Young and William Cowper, two representative poets of the period.

Edward Young, remembered as an imitator of the style of Alexander Pope, places commerce among the highest of the arts, or at least among the highest in terms of its beneficial effects on mankind. In his work *Imperium Pelagi* (1730) we find this passage, from the section entitled "The Merchant."

> Commerce brings fair riches; riches crown
> Fair virtue with the first renown.
> A large revenue, and a large expense,
> When hearts for others' welfare glow,
> And spend as free as gods bestow,
> Gives the full bloom to mortal excellence.[18]

As trade expands, expenditures expand with it and this improves the welfare of all. This process opens up the heart of man and, consequently, improves his inner life.

But Young does not stop with the inner man. Another great and wonderful effect of trade is the carrying of the benefits of civilization throughout the world. The drive for personal gain results in global benefits.

> Commerce gives Arts, as well as gain:
> By Commerce wafted o'er the main,
> They barbarous climes enlighten as they run.
> Arts, the rich traffic of the soul,
> May travel thus from pole to pole,
> And gild the world with Learning's brighter sun.[19]

Having dealt with man, his soul, and civilization, Young goes even higher and moves his thoughts toward the bosom of creation itself.

> Kings, merchants are in league and love;
> Earth's odours play soft airs above,
> That o'er the teeming field prolific range.
> Planets are merchants; take, return,
> Lustre and heat; by traffic burn:
> The whole creation is one vast Exchange.[20]

Coming back down toward earth, Young lauds the human mover of all this, the trader. "Who studies trade, he studies all; /Accomplish'd merchants are accomplish'd men."[21] Man, society, even the world, are fulfilled by trade. What more could be said for economic man?

William Cowper, that great but unbalanced admirer of nature who anticipated Wordsworth, also had some thoughts on trade, and they are similar to Young's. In his poem "Charity" (1782) he alludes to the divine social plan which "By various ties attaches man to man."[22] One of these ties is trade. Nature's rich and varied endowments are dispersed unevenly over the globe. As a result, each part of the earth lacks what the other parts produce. Trade solves this problem.

> Each climate needs what other climes produce,
> And offers something to the gen'ral use;
> No land but listens to the common call,
> And in return receives supply from all.[23]

Cowper next sees civilization, through the development of trade, coming to improve the character of man.

> This genial intercourse, and mutual aid,
> Cheers what were else an universal shade,
> Calls nature from her ivy mantled den,
> And softens human rock-work into men.
> Ingenious Art, with her expressive face,
> Steps forth to fashion and refine the race.[24]

Nature and man are softened and refined by commerce. For Young and Cowper, the personal, social, global, even metaphysical, credentials of economic man could hardly be higher.

Of course, not all eighteenth-century writers showed such effusive praise for trade and the character of economic man. Some very critical voices were heard. These criticisms were usually selective, concentrating on certain specific business practices of the period. They seldom were a broad or comprehensive condemnation of trade or traders. Some of these criticisms were new, others old. Some anticipated the scathing attacks on economic man to come later, in the nineteenth century, when the social conditions produced by the industrial revolution prompted such strong reactions.

Josiah Tucker, dean of Gloucester and controversialist on many topics, repeats a long-standing attack against monopolists, who are, after all, men of trade even though their immense economic power often lifts them above the concerns of ordinary economic men. In his *The Elements of Commerce and Theory of Taxes* (1755) he identifies the human motive of self-love as "the great Mover of created beings." But Tucker sees a problem connected with this drive. If it is not controlled, it tends to defeat its own ends. The reason for this, he explains, is that, by its very nature, "Self-love is narrow and confined in its Views, and admits of no *Sharers* and *Competitors*."[25] Even if this drive carries individuals so far as to form combinations and exclusive societies to serve their common interest, each remains in competition with the others. All such groups, he argues, must eventually end in mutual poverty for their members. Monopolists cannot stand other members of their monopoly and so set out to destroy each other. Self-interest leads to self-destructing monopolies, which serve neither the interest of businessmen nor that of the public. It would appear that Tucker's monopolies would disappear in time as self-interest tears them apart. But he is not willing to wait; he hates any concentration of economic power simply and directly. Monopolies are bad in themselves. But, to make the situation worse, Tucker complains, "Monopolies are formed and *Charters* granted under the ridiculous and absurd Pretense of the Public Good, when, in Fact, private Advantage is the only Point aimed at."[26] He equates monopoly with knavery.[27]

Tucker puts the large landowner in the class of the monopolist. By tying people to the land and confining their labor to menial tasks in order to serve his own interest, the landowner impedes improvements in agriculture. At the same time, he stands in the way of his workers improving their own condition. His self-interest hurts the welfare in general as it hurts the individual in particular. So the landowner "in the Landed Interest is just the same kind of Monster as an *Exclusive* Company in the Commercial: They are both Monopolists . . . and their chief Wealth consists rather in preventing others from acquiring Wealth, than in being rich themselves."[28] Self-interest, Tucker maintains, can be made to serve the public welfare only when any business activity is free for all to enter. This condition, unfortunately, has not yet arrived, for, he says, "we still want the Glorious Revolution in the Commercial System, which we have happily obtained in the Political."[29]

Tucker's general assault on monopoly gets down to cases when he takes up many of the large British trading companies to show the public harm they do. He castigates the following famous trading companies with some of the sharpest invective of his time: Turkey, Hudson's Bay, East-India, and South-Sea.[30] Economic man has too large an ego; it is good neither for the public nor for himself. His exclusiveness leads to poverty both public and private.

We can feel Tucker's outrage toward the monopolist in the writing of Adam Smith but it is now more controlled and, therefore, more incisive. Smith will be taken up in later chapters as we approach his work from a different point of view, but some of his negative remarks about the character of the businessman are worth mentioning at this point. One of the most widely quoted passages from the *Wealth of Nations* (1776) is, "People of the same trade seldom meet together . . . but the conversation ends in a conspiracy against the public, or in some contrivance to raise prices."[31] Smith emphasizes the deceptive practices of business as he refers to "the clamour and sophistry of merchants and manufacturers" in their attempts to convince the people of the countryside that the special economic privileges of the towns are really in "the general interest of the whole."[32] He also mentions how employers manipulate their workmen, how they "enflame their workmen, to attack with violence and outrage" any proposals for freer trade. Smith likens these workers to an "overgrown standing army" which has become formidable to the government, using its raw power to abuse, insult, and even threaten with real danger any member of the legislature opposing the policies of their employers.[33]

But Smith saves his most scathing comments for those members of Parliament who display the base attitudes of businessmen when they should be formulating laws appropriate to the policies of a great empire. Some members of Parliament argue, for example, that, because Portugal is a better customer for British goods than France, Britain should buy her wine from Portugal rather than from France. Smith's sharp comment on this kind of pleading makes his position on the matter unmistakable. "The sneaking arts of underling tradesmen are thus erected into political maxims for the conduct of a great empire." While he realizes it is too much to expect that the political ambitions of kings and ministers will not disrupt trade, Smith hopes, at least, that "the mean rapacity, the monopolizing spirit of merchants and manufacturers" would be prevented from doing so.[34] The spirit of monopoly, "the interested sophistry of merchants and manufacturers [has] confounded the common sense of mankind,"[35] Smith concludes.

Adam Smith's criticism of economic man is directed at that man's mean and narrow policies toward trade. But there is in the *Wealth of Nations* an important economic principle based upon the facts and realities of production that is not connected with arguable points of policy. This is the principle of the division of labor. Smith more than any previous writer emphasized this principle, which he looked upon as the prime mover in the economic development of nations. Specialization does improve productive efficiency; this is a technical fact, not a point of debate. But an advanced division of labor reduces work to simple and repetitive tasks. The resulting effect on labor is a point of debate. Smith and others were aware that extreme specialization of labor could stultify the worker.[36] The businessman, in his role of promoting the division of labor, might, possibly, be attacked for these bad effects on labor. Smith chose not to do so. But William Godwin, our next writer, most certainly did make such an attack.

Godwin in his *Political Justice* (1798) approached economic problems from the comprehensive viewpoint of the moral philosopher, not as a "scientific" investigator, the type who was about to emerge with the newly arrived discipline of political economy. He believed that mankind could eventually reach a state of perfection. But before this could happen man would have to eliminate the avaricious element in his character. Unfortunately, Godwin notes, "The division of labor . . . is the offspring of avarice."[37] He then refers to Smith's famed example of the principle at work in a pin factory, where output is increased many times by its use. Calling this "refinement" in the methods of production as "the growth of monopoly," Godwin claims the "object is, to see into how vast a surface the industry of the lower classes may be beaten, the more completely to gild over the indolent and the proud."[38] To Godwin, the division of labor is simply a device to enrich the powerful at the expense of labor. He makes very clear his estimation of the profit motive in man. "All wealth, in a state of civilized society, is the produce of human industry," he maintains. But in society, as currently organized, the "landed proprietor first takes a very disproportionate share of the produce to himself; the capitalist follows, and shows himself equally voracious."[39] Little is left for the worker whose industry is the source of the wealth in the first place. Godwin's indictment of economic man is severe, showing him to be motivated by the basest of desires and also to be a direct exploiter of his laborers. In this indictment, Godwin anticipates the class-oriented assault on businessmen, which will become so common in the following century.

So far, we have seen several sides to the personality of economic man. He is thrifty and industrious, worldly and eloquent, contented and well-disposed. He is the carrier of civilization to the world and even a kind of fulfiller of cosmic destiny. On the other hand, he is a narrow and confining monopolist who conspires with others of his ilk to exploit his customers as he tries to debase the policies of great nations. Finally, he is the degrader and exploiter of his workers. These assaults on the character of economic man will continue and intensify, for we have now reached the nineteenth century, the age of industrialism.

If any age belongs to economic man then surely it must be the nineteenth century. For hundreds of years prior to this time the British landscape had altered very little. Cathedral spires rose during the age of faith but merely as points of emphasis in a largely unchanging picture. With the nineteenth century, however, the very texture and color of things radically changed with the arrival of factories, railroads, furnaces, and all the rest of the sprawling apparatus of industrialism. Even the air changed in color and texture as the smoke of industrialism filled the skies. All of the works of the great builders of history hardly compare to the works of economic man during this age of high industrialism. Economic man had, indeed, reached his heroic age.

Modern economic man was, at this time, being closely observed by certain scholars and intellectuals, and his activities were influencing their ideas. The result was the new science of political economy and it was used, largely, to explain and justify his existence. It is one thing to have an occasional poet or essayist commend your character and works to his readers. It is something else to have writers of heavy and complex tomes acting as your full-time professional advocates. This was economic man's enviable position in the early decades of the nineteenth century, with the establishment of the school of classical economics. Religions, philosophies, political systems all had enjoyed their apologists in the past. Now economic man had his apologists, too.

The classical economists reduced economic life to several basic and inescapable laws, that of diminishing returns being the single most important. These laws, they maintained, had a validity similar to the validity of the physical sciences. The result was a science of inevitabilities over-spreading not only the materials and processes in the production and distribution of wealth but also the worker himself. They saw labor as subject to the laws controlling higher-level economic processes. The key figure in all this is economic man, for he initiates the processes of indus-trialism. He gathers the resources, organizes them, sets the whole indus-trial apparatus into motion, and acts as the conductor of business life. It was the century of economic man not only in a material sense but, now, also in an intellectual sense.

When a movement reaches its height, a reaction often sets in, and the reaction to nineteenth-century economic man and his learned advocates was very strong, indeed.[40] We will begin with Thomas Carlyle, for no other writer equals him in the vigor and color of his language as he assaults economic man. Referring, facetiously, to major business leaders as "Captains of Industry,"[41] Carlyle ridicules them for the baseness of their motives and values. "Bobus Higgins, Sausage-maker on the great scale . . . what is it that you . . . pay reverence to?" Carlyle answers: "cash-accounts and larders dropping fatness."[42] And "The indomitable Plugson too, of the respected Firm of Plugson, Hunks and Company," is invited by Carlyle to reflect on the following: "Bookkeeping by double entry is admirable, and records several things in an exact manner." But, Carlyle notes, "the Mother-Destinies also keep their Tablets . . . and the statement and balance . . . in the Plugson Ledgers and on the Tablets of Heaven's Chancery are discrepant exceedingly."[43] Richard Arkwright will have his monument, Carlyle claims: "all Lancashire and Yorkshire . . . with their machineries and industries. . . . A true *pyramid* or '*flame-mountain*', flaming with steam fires . . . —how much grander than your foolish Cheops Pyramids or Sakhara clay ones!"[44] And the American businessman? "My friend, brag not yet of our American cousins! Their quantity of cotton, dollars, industry and resources, I believe to be almost unspeakable. . . ." But at the same time America has produced "Eighteen Millions of the greatest *bores* ever seen in this world before."[45]

In spite of this invective, Carlyle shows a degree of grudging admira-tion for his "Captains of Industry" because, if nothing else, they are leaders of men. This accords with Carlyle's very high opinion of heroes. One of the social problems of his day was mass unemployment, and Carlyle feels there is a pressing need to organize the unemployed. He looks to the businessman to accomplish this task because he has talents for commanding men. If businessmen are "Captains" of the employed, why not appoint them leaders of the unemployed? They will know how to put them to work.

Carlyle saves his strongest assaults for the early classical economists and other less rigorous but vocal supporters of economic man, lumping them together under the derisive title "Professors of the Dismal Science."[46] He finds the intellectual mentors of this group back among the eighteenth-century "Scottish sages" whose conception of life, Carlyle claims, "shows neither briers nor roses; but only a flat, continuous thrashing-floor for logic, whereon all questions, from the 'Doctrine of Rent' to the 'Natural History of Religion', are thrashed and sifted with the same mechanical impartiality!"[47] Attacking the dominant economic doctrine of laissez-faire, with its emphasis on self-interest and opposition to government intervention in trade, Carlyle describes how this doctrine maintains that nothing can be done or should be done about the trade cycle; how idle factories and idle workers should wait quietly for the turn in the cycle and for trade and employment to revive. He ridicules this doctrine by calling it "Paralytic Radicalism . . . which gauges with Statistic measuring-reed, sounds with Philosophic Politico-Economic plummet the deep dark sea of troubles." Having concluded what "an infinite sea of troubles it is," the doctrine turns over the cure to "time and general laws." It then, "without so much as recommending suicide, coldly takes its leave of us."[48] Carlyle caustically replies to the supporters of this doctrine: "Let Paralysis retire to secret places . . . the public highways ought not to be occupied by people demonstrating that motion is impossible."[49]

Carlyle utterly rejects the idea that free and uncontrolled private interests will work in harmony and further the public welfare. The argument that the drive of men's self-interest can be curbed by competition, by external market forces, rather than by internal curbs on appetites, he finds absurd. He accuses the classical economists of trying to replace virtue with mechanics. Strangely, he says, they claim "checking and balancing, and other adjustments of Profit and Loss" will guide men "to their true advantage."[50] This "gospel of 'Enlightened Selfishness',"[51] in which "going to Hell is the equivalent of not making money,"[52] where the "word *Soul* . . . seems to be synonymous with *Stomach*,"[53] may be all right for "Human Beavers pretending to be Men,"[54] but real men will have other ideas. Carlyle deplores his age as one of "Anarchy *plus* a constable!"[55]

Carlyle's indictment of the age of industrialism does not stop with economic man and his intellectual supporters. He is also struck by what industrialism has done to the British countryside. "The huge demon of Mechanism smokes and thunders, panting at his great task, in all sections of English land . . . *oversetting* whole multitudes of workmen . . . hurling them asunder . . . so that the wisest no longer knows his whereabout." The "giant Steam engine in a giant English Nation will here create violent demand for labour, and will there annihilate demand."[56]

A number of the ideas and images used by Carlyle in his broad attack on

23

industrialism can be seen again in Charles Dicken's novel *Hard Times* (1854–55). In this work Dickens delineates economic man more sharply than ever. He does this by taking some of the personal traits of economic man and dividing them between two of his leading characters. Economic man in an industrial setting must command vast amounts of materials and a large number of men. Therefore, he must be pushing and physical. Dickens gives these characteristics to Josiah Bounderby, a very successful industrialist operating on a considerable scale. But the more interesting traits of economic man Dickens gives to Thomas Gradgrind, who also came up through business, but now devotes his energies to education and politics as he preaches a gospel of facts and practicalness while he denigrates feelings and emotions. Gradgrind is the cerebral side of economic man. Bounderby overwhelms everyone around him with endless stories about his struggles in climbing from the gutter to the top. He drowns all near him with floods of himself. Gradgrind, in contrast, listens to others but only to detect any emotions lurking in their characters. If he finds any, he tries to root them out and to replace them with facts—hard, industrial facts. In a world where everything is weighed and measured, he insists there is no place for personal feelings. Both characters, or parts of the personality of economic man, have the same goal, a world safe for realities and practicalities. Their aim is a world of "nothing but Facts!" as Dickens put it in the opening paragraphs of *Hard Times*.

Bounderby, the "Bully of Humility," is a survivor. He enters the novel as a hard, insensitive primitive and leaves it exactly the same way, completely unscathed by the personal crises of the other characters around him. Clearly, Dickens feels that this side of economic man cannot be redeemed. But Gradgrind is not made of such strong material. He is devoted to his missionary work for facts in the schools. He closely supervises the education of his children, two of whom are named after Adam Smith and Thomas Malthus, in order that the concrete and the real will fill their minds to the exclusion of color and affection. He gains a seat in Parliament to carry his practical philosophy there. But in the end he is brought down by the failure that two of his children make of their lives. He realizes that it was caused by the false values he had imposed on them.

This story about the downfall of economic man fittingly takes place in Coketown, which Dickens describes as full of machinery, smoke, and noise. The working population is as dull and uniform as its buildings and streets. Life rubs along as the machinery does, and with no more purpose. Dickens places economic man in the stupefying hell of industrialism, divides his soul in two, and shows that the sensitive and potentially better part cannot survive.

John Ruskin, our final commentator on the character of economic man, sees *Hard Times* as an important work but one in which Dickens has obscured his message with overuse of dramatics. He feels that the novel has been diminished by use of "colour and caricature" and, because its subject is of great national importance, he wishes that Dickens had used a "severer and more accurate analysis."[57] Dickens's hearty style and use of exaggeration does not sit well with Ruskin's more finely tuned feelings.

Ruskin brings a more sensitive mind to the problems of economic man and industrialism than any we have yet seen. A Carlyle or a Dickens is able to stand up to the vulgarities and crudities of Victorian business life and almost seem to thrive in attacking them. The flush of battle seems to carry them through, even though, in the end, the battle may be lost. But with Ruskin the excitement of battle is not enough. His attacks on economic man and his works eventually fade and tail off into a deep pessimism. He brings much more fragile feelings to the problem than do Carlyle and Dickens.

Ruskin sees the main problem of his age as the quality of life. The way that man makes his living is best judged by how it affects the lives of people involved in it. Production and consumption are best judged by what kind of a life they impose on the worker and the consumer, and this cannot be measured in terms of absolutes independent of humane values. Wealth is relative; in judging its true value everything depends on the kind of wealth it is, where it is located, and how it is used. Wealth can never be a measure in itself and of itself. A true science of wealth should consider, for example, what is "the right thing to the right man," which, Ruskin adds, is "dependent on more than arithmetic."[58] Wealth produced in the wrong way or in the wrong quantities debases what is human in the character of man. Economic man and his supporters in classical economics, Ruskin argues, are completely unaware of these important facts.

While both production and consumption present challenges, Ruskin feels that "wise consumption is a far more difficult art than wise production." The "vital question, for individual and nation, is, never 'how much do they make?' but 'to what purpose do they spend?'"[59] And because classical economics ignores this important point, "I have fearlessly declared your so-called science of Political Economy to be no science; because, namely, it has omitted the study of exactly the most important branch of the business—the study of *spending*."[60] Ruskin does not deny a certain kind of "truth" to the theories of classical economics; given its "terms," its conclusions follow. But, he says, "I am simply uninterested in them [the terms], as I should be in those of a science of gymnastics which assumed that men had no skeletons. . . . I simply deny its applicability to the present phase of the world."[61] Ruskin sees America as a place where "your model science of political economy [is] brought to its perfect practice." It is a place of "every man for himself," of "vulgar faith in magnitude and multitude," of "perpetual self-contemplation . . . frantic with hope of

25

uncomprehended change, and progress they know not whither."[62] In sum, Ruskin describes the science of political economy as "the weighing of clouds, and the portioning out of shadows."[63]

Ruskin is appalled by the appearances of industrialism. His artistic temperament is in revolt as he comments bitterly, "All England may, if it chooses, become one manufacturing town; and Englishmen sacrificing themselves to the good of general humanity, may live diminished lives in the midst of noise, of darkness, and of deadly exhalation."[64] He describes London as "that great foul city . . . rattling, growling, smoking, stinking,— a ghastly heap of fermenting brickwork, pouring poison at every pore."[65] And finally, despondently, he refers to Carlyle's voice as "the only faithful and useful utterance in all England, and [it] has sounded through all these years in vain!"[66]

So much for the personality and works of economic man. We have seen him as a Puritan, a worldly ascetic hoarding up hours of labor for the credit of his soul to God. He has been the cosmopolitan Sir Andrew Freeport, whose interesting conversation makes him attractive company and whose daily activities need not be put in the shade by those of any gentleman. He has been Defoe's busy and therefore happy craftsman or trader, who so much more pleasantly fills his hours than does the laggard. But economic man also has a darker side. Tucker sees him driven toward monopoly, and eventually poverty, by the insatiable appetite of self-interest. Smith describes his devious and conspiratorial nature and his corrupting influence on the economic policies of a great nation. Godwin finds him to be a rapacious exploiter of the laboring poor. Carlyle, with mordant raillery, ridicules the meanness of his interests, his calculating and utilitarian character. Dickens outlines strongly his primitive and thrusting nature on the one side, while emphasizing his cold and unemotional character on the other. For Ruskin economic man is the inhuman destroyer of those things giving meaning and quality to life.

What is the universal or fundamental element in the personality of economic man? What is it in his makeup that cannot be removed if he is to remain what he is? The answer is self-interest. This is the one drive that is common to all our writers' depictions of economic man. Whether economic man is the introspective Puritan, the extroverted man of the world, the cold calculator of gain, the conspirator, the manipulator, or even the primitive destroyer, his underlying motive is self-interest. Our writers have either placed this characteristic of economic man in the foreground of their comments or they have assumed it to be so obvious that they have handled it in an implicit manner. In any event it is that feature of economic man which cannot be removed if he is to remain economic man.

Replace the generous nature of a Freeport with the confined character of a Gradgrind, or the openness of Defoe's craftsman with the narrowness of a Puritan, or trade the cramped streets and smoky alleys of Coketown for routes on the open sea, and self-interest remains the same. Self-interest is the constant; it cannot be removed and replaced with any other element in his character. Self-interest is the soul of economic man.

The word "soul" has a number of meanings and it has been applied both in abstract and material senses to describe any number of things. It has very strong individualistic meanings having to do with self, meanings that apply to the deepest part of one's inner personality. But the word has also been used in a social context. It has often been applied to groups to describe what animates them. An individual may be, for example, a "soul of discretion" but mobs, armies, institutions, even whole cultures have been accorded "souls" by many writers. It is a word having both personal and collective meanings.

A person may judge his own inner motives strictly from his own viewpoint on a purely individualistic basis. But groups of people, in fact whole societies, also scrutinize the inner motives of individuals and pass judgment on them too. Our interest in the soul of economic man is in this second way, in how his drive of self-interest was scrutinized and judged by society. In our time period, from Thomas Hobbes to Adam Smith, those who judged the motive of self-interest for society were largely moral philosophers and theologians. As noted earlier, they are to be the main characters in this work. I plan to show how these arbiters of social values took up the idea of self-interest, examined it from many sides, argued and debated it, and eventually concluded that the self-interested actions of the individual were conducive to, even necessary, for the public welfare. But first, we must examine the thought of Thomas Hobbes, for it is he more than any other who, originally, stimulated these discussions of self-interest.

3
Thomas Hobbes
Self-Interest and the Public Destruction

And Covenants, without the Sword, are but Words. . . .
                                                    Thomas Hobbes

The distance between Thomas Hobbes and Adam Smith, both in time and ideas, is indeed a long one. But the century separating them seems hardly long enough to account for the radical changes in attitudes toward the idea of self-interest which occurred. At the beginning, Hobbes stated in the most certain terms that mankind could expect only the darkest results from the free operation of self-interest. In contrast, toward the end of this period the thoughts of several writers soar upward when contemplating the social effects of self-interest. These later writers penned philosophic rhapsodies to self-interest as they looked to the principle as the source of culture and civilization. Slightly later, Adam Smith also wrote about the positive results that could be expected from freer opportunities for self-interest. He did not use the florid rhetoric of these earlier writers, but in his methodical way he argued that unfettered self-interest could have clearly beneficial results, such as thriving economies and a more comfortable level of living for mankind. Smith confined his study of self-interest largely to its material effects. He felt little need to consider the effects of self-interest in higher terms. During this period, the idea of self-interest carried minds all the way from Hobbes's visions of death and destruction, through anticipations of the perfected society, and finally to Smith's positive but somewhat restrained expectations of increasing comfort for mankind.

Hobbes saw self-interest as a prime mover among the various motives in natural man and he emphasized its great personal and social importance. He also saw it as the most destructive of human motives. This great importance he attached to self-interest and his very harsh view of it attracted the attention of other writers, caused strong reactions, and forced them to give serious consideration to the principle. Much of their time was spent in refuting Hobbes's positions on self-interest, and we will find, in these refutations, anticipations of certain important eighteenth-century ideas about self-interest. So Hobbes is important for attracting

28

serious attention to the principle of self-interest, and for inducing minds to come forth with new ideas about the principle.

Another reason for starting with Hobbes is that he suggested two categories for studying the implications of self-interest, the material and the mental. We will see that later writers will follow this distinction in their treatments of the principle. Some will approach self-interest largely from the materialistic point of view, one which examines the real or economic effects of the principle. Others will see self-interest largely in psychological terms, or as a human motive, and will study how this motive fits in with other drives in man's character. And a few writers will mix the two categories and consider both the material and mental effects of self-interest at the same time.

The problem of self-interest and its relation to the public welfare seems to be a relatively modern one. Considering the modernity of Hobbes as a thinker, it seems appropriate that he should have been so vitally concerned with the issue.[1] Whether Hobbes can be considered a modern thinker because he was concerned with a modern problem or whether it is the reverse, a modern problem creating modernity of thought in a leading mind, need not detain us. The point is that Hobbes struggled with a problem that has come down to us in the twentieth century, a problem that has been a focal point of debate during much of modern history. And, as yet, it has not been fully resolved either in theory or practice.

Hobbes's view of the character of natural man leaves no room for delicate feeling or sentiment. To him, man reacts to circumstances only from narrow considerations of self. Hobbes's life may afford some explanation for this hard and unrelenting interpretation of man. He was born prematurely in 1588 because, it was said, his mother was terrified at the news of the approaching Spanish Armada. (Commenting about the events of his birth, Hobbes said that he and fear were born twins.) Showing early promise as a scholar, he was sent to Oxford in 1603 but was not awarded his B.A. degree until 1608. After Oxford, he became associated with the Cavendish family and the relationship became very close, lasting almost his entire life. His connection with the family afforded time for study and writing and also the opporunity to meet and talk with some of the leading minds of his day. Hobbes gradually developed a reputation among scholars and writers, and his absolutist views became generally known. When, in 1640, Charles I was forced for fiscal reasons to convene Parliament, a Parliament whose members were opposed to his strongly centralist policies, Hobbes feared for his own safety, because of his reputation for support of authority, and left for France. Now free from the threat of parliamentary attacks for his royalist views, he continued his discussions and writing on philosophical questions as he spent considerable time with intellectuals on the Continent. Later, in the same decade, he became associated with the royal exiles from the British Civil War and for a short period was mathematical tutor to the Prince of Wales. But he seems to have fallen out of favor with the royal household and, fearing that French authorities might prosecute him for atheism, he returned to England in 1651 where he remained the rest of his life.

Hobbes's fear and suspicions about the intentions of men of power toward him were reinforced by other incidents late in his life. In 1665 the plague swept London and fire destroyed much of the city in the following year. Some said that these disasters were a sign of divine wrath, and that the cause was rampant atheism. A bill was brought before Parliament for suppression of atheism, containing provisions to investigate the book *Leviathan* (1651), Hobbes's most famous work. The bill was eventually dropped but the threat was plain. The king also acted against another of Hobbes's works, *Behemoth* (1668), by initially forbidding its publication. And the authorities of the church prohibited, for a time, the reprinting of *Leviathan*. Hobbes was convinced that men of power knew no limits to their designs on the lives of other men, but he lived vigorously to an extremely old age, dying in 1679.

Hobbes was born with fear, he fled to France from fear, and he was forced to retreat to England because of his fear of French authorities. He saw the British state dissolve into the chaos of civil war as suspicion mounted about the king's intentions toward property and religion. Hobbes's earliest published work on the nature of society and the necessary conditions for stable and secure government, *De Cive* (1642 in Latin and 1651 in English translation), was written, he said, so that "you will no longer suffer ambitious men through streams of your blood to wade to their own power."[2] He also saw his *Leviathan* as "occasioned by the disorders of the present time."[3] If Hobbes had lived through more settled and peaceful times and had never felt the threat of civil and ecclesiastical authority he still might have entertained similar opinions about the aggressiveness of man and still might have supported the need for strong central authority. But it is evident that his life and times, being what they were, probably strengthened an already hard and astringent view of life.

Hobbes's conception of the basic nature of man is thoroughly materialistic. As is common among many social theorists of the seventeenth and eighteenth centuries, he begins his study of man by stripping away the disguising and obscuring paraphernalia of social life in order to see man in his natural and essential state. Hobbes removes man from institutions and customs, hoping to see him as he really is. His method might, in a sense, be likened to the mathematical because he is subtracting elements from what makes up the totality of man's condition and nature, the remainder being the denominator common to all individuals.[4] He intends to get down to the irreducible in man. After taking all else away, Hobbes finds that, at base, life is motion. This is an inescapable fact which must be dealt with before any valid knowledge can be gained about the social nature of man. Man is momentum. This is the starting point for Hobbes's entire theory of society.

He says, very directly, that "life is but a motion of Limbs" and, in another place, "Life it selfe is but Motion."[5] He then adds an important feature to his idea of motion and this is the then recently discovered principle of inertia, or the physical property of bodies to continue to move once they have been set in motion. As Hobbes put it, "when a thing is in motion, it will eternally be in motion, unless somewhat els stay it."[6] He seems to have no hesitation in applying this new principle of physics directly to man. Man's motion is absolute, continuing of its own accord until something outside man deflects or stops it. Hobbes refers to motional man in a number of places in his works but his most apt description occurs in his likening of life to a race. He also uses this parallel in order to identify and describe the various human passions because, ultimately, these passions arise from the motion that is life. "The comparison of the life of man to a race," Hobbes writes, "though it hold not in every part, yet it holdeth so well for our purpose, that we may thereby both see and remember almost all the passions." He notes that the race of life has no final goal other than "being foremost, and in it." The race, not the arrival, matters. I will quote only some of the twenty-five couplings he makes between actions in the race and their appropriate passions.

> To endeavor, is *appetite.*
> To consider them behind, is *glory.*
> To consider them before, is *humility.*
> To lose ground with looking back, *vain glory.*
>
> .   .   .   .
>
> To be in breath, *hope.*
> To be weary, *despair.*
>
> .   .   .   .
>
> To break through a sudden stop, *anger.*
> To break through with ease, *magnamimity.*
>
> .   .   .   .
>
> To see another fall, is disposition to *laugh.*
>
> .   .   .   .
>
> And to forsake the course, is to *die.*[7]

Natural man's innate motion manifests itself in several ways. First, in the form of competition. Because all men have roughly equal abilities, both in body and in mind, any man can claim for himself benefits which any other may desire. The result is animosity because, as Hobbes explains, "From this equality of ability, ariseth equality of hope in the attaining of our Ends. And therefore if any two men desire the same thing, which nevertheless they cannot both enjoy, they become enemies."[8] Second, motion manifests itself as distrust. Out of competition comes deep suspicions about the intentions of others. This leads to attempts at personal domination in order to secure safety or, as Hobbes put it, "to master the persons of all men he can, so long, till he see no other power great enough to endanger him."[9] Finally, man's innate motion comes out as the seeking of glory, because "every man looketh that his companion should value him, at the same rate he sets upon himselfe."[10]

Hobbes summarizes these results of natural man's motion in the starkest of terms. Because every man is an enemy to every other, there is no security. Without security there can be little or no time for learning and industry. Natural man, therefore, lacks knowledge, arts, letters, even society, and, as Hobbes sums up in a much-quoted phrase, "And the life of man [is] solitary, poore, nasty, brutish, and short."[11]

In his natural state, Hobbes maintains, "every man has a Right to every thing"[12] or a "right of all to all."[13] And, because man is insatiably acquisitive, "that right of all men to all things, is in effect no better than if no man had right to any thing."[14] Collective rights negate individual rights. It follows, Hobbes reasons, that in this condition "of every man against every man, this is also consequent; that nothing can be Unjust. The notions of Right and Wrong, Justice and Injustice have there no place."[15] Social standards of proper behavior do not exist because society does not exist.

But man need not remain in this brutish state if he will use his reason. It is clear that men should seek peace. In order to gain peace, Hobbes says, each man must renounce his right to everything. This can take place when every individual gives up his own rights by transferring them to another man or to an assembly of men. Out of this process of mass conferring of rights a new and sovereign power comes into being, an artificial being containing the powers of all individual men, a "great Leviathan." Here, again, Hobbes seems to be reasoning mathematically, as he adds the powers of individuals together to arrive at a total power greater than any of its parts. The device used in this summing of powers is that of the contract. The individual transfers his power to the new civil authority on the condition that the authority use its great strength to enforce peace. With peace attained, men can effectively transact business among themselves because they now can expect agreements to be kept. A power now exists to enforce such agreements. In the state of nature, bonds between men amount to nothing but words, for there is no overriding power to enforce them. As Hobbes puts it succinctly, "And Covenants, without the Sword, are but Words."[16] Fear and distrust of other men subside as the state acts as a great disciplinarian. Property can now be accumulated because its owner can feel secure in its possession. As Hobbes explains, "*Propriety* is an effect of Common-wealth."[17]

The power of the state must be absolute for, as Hobbes puts it, the state is "King of the Proud,"[18] and pride is a passion very difficult to control. The fundamental drive of self-interest still poses a threat to peace. As property is accumulated, such a threat may increase, for Hobbes associates property with power. He therefore takes a stand against accumulations of property sufficiently large for their owners to entertain pretensions against the power of civil authority. In that property exists only because of the preserving presence of the sovereign power, it "is not to be pretended against the same," he argues. Consequently, "Those levies therefore which are made upon men's estates . . . are no more but the price of peace and defense which the sovereignty maintaineth for them."[19] The taxing power of the state is the price paid to maintain private property. It is abundantly clear that Hobbes places the necessities of state power ahead of the rights of private property. Following this same line of thought, he shows suspicions of monopolies, corporations, and other concentrations of private economic power, for they can be potential threats to the power of the state. He refers to corporations as "many lesser Common-wealths in the bowels of a greater, like wormes in the entrayles of a naturall man."[20] He makes the point, implicitly, that such lesser powers should not be allowed to grow so large as to endanger the health of the commonwealth.

Hobbes says that it is a law of nature "*That one man allow commerce and traffic indifferently to one another*."[21] He feels this is necessary to avoid any discrimination which might lead to contention and, eventually, to a threat to peace. This stand for free entry into markets might be interpreted as favoring a policy which works to restrain the already economically powerful. This is not to imply that Hobbes was a thoroughgoing free trader or that he appreciated the full implications of a free-trade policy. He seems to have some awareness of the fact that peaceful competition can exert some degree of control over private economic power. But the intensity of competition must be limited because, otherwise, man would fall back into his original chaotic state. So the state must remain all-powerful. This can hardly be called a policy of economic liberalism.

Hobbes definitely favors policies to preserve and enhance the power of the state. If this means increasing its power directly by what appears to be an almost unlimited power to tax, so be it. Or, if it means increasing its power relatively, by reducing or containing the size of lesser centers of power, Hobbes is for this too. Economic freedom for the individual is possible but only well below the absolute freedom of the state. The state must be the monitor of man's actions in self-interest.

The civil power, according to Hobbes, is absolute, but it is not created as an end in itself. It exists to direct the drive of self-interest into constructive lines. Primitive, presocial self-interest leads to confusion and disorder, but limited self-interest operating under the iron rules imposed by state power promotes the public welfare. "Civil society," Hobbes explains, is not sought "for its own sake, but that we may receive some honour or profit from it,"[22] or, as he says in another place, "when we voluntarily contract society . . . we look after the object of the will, that is, that, which every one . . . propounds to himself for good."[23] He then goes on to explain that "whatsoever seems good . . . is pleasant, and relates either to the senses, or the mind."[24] The things catering to the senses Hobbes calls "conveniences," which are the materials serving the physical needs of man. But the things catering to the pleasure of the mind are far less tangible. He identifies them as the attaining of "glory," or having "a good opinion of one's self." "All society," he concludes, "therefore is either for gain, or for glory; that is, not so much for love of our fellows, as for love of ourselves."[25] In short, society exists only to serve the ends of self-interest, either in material or mental terms.

If we go back for a moment to Hobbes's natural state of man, it is clear that neither gain nor glory can be attained under this condition. Where a right by all to all prevails, material gain is limited or practically impossible. And subsisting in a state of perpetual fear and suspicion is hardly conducive to visions of glory. Self-interest gone wild is the ruin of man's existence but, if he will use his reason, this drive can lead to his salvation as it spurs him into constructing an authority powerful enough to curb the drive's excesses. With self-interest under control, mankind can begin to realize the good that can come out of this drive. But the price is absolute government.

Hobbes, it is clear, entertained a most jaundiced view of the basic nature of man. In order for man to reach any acceptable level of life he must submit to an external and all-powerful authority. Hobbes saw nothing in the soul of man, on a purely individualistic basis, strong enough to contain the destructive drive of self-interest. It was impossible for the individual working with his own inner resources to bring his own self-interest under control. Such was the dismal state of man.

But is man so inherently wilful that he must either subsist miserably or submit to absolute authority? Certain writers thought not. They looked with abhorrence on Hobbes's view of man and thought his analysis unrealistic.

II
SOLUTIONS FROM ON HIGH

4
Richard Cumberland
Self-Interest and the Principle of Design

It is vain to expect that a bad Man will become a good Subject.

Richard Cumberland

As the outlines of Hobbes's doctrines began to emerge clearly there developed what was to be a debate, with Hobbes on one side and the Cambridge Platonists and Bishop Richard Cumberland on the other.[1] The Cambridge Platonists, a group whose prominent members were John Smith, Ralph Cudworth, Henry More, and Benjamin Whichcote, were among those reacting most adversely to the ideas of Hobbes. Several of the group were trained at or associated with Emmanuel College at Cambridge, an intellectual stronghold for Puritanism. These men are usually connected with the latitudinarian movement or the attempt to move Protestant thought beyond the rigid and unbending dogmas of Calvinist theology toward greater flexibility and moderation. There was among the Cambridge Platonists a belief in the value of contemplation and meditation, of quiet efforts by the individual to discover moral law by inspecting the resources of his own mind.

Hobbes, in contrast, had insisted that the essence of life is motion, that men are, more than anything else, bodies in movement. This movement lacked a systematic pattern; it was uncontrolled and resulted in random collisions with other men. When this crashing about and into one another became intolerable, Hobbes argued, men would be forced to consult their reason and agree to construct an artificial body of absolute authority. This authority would promulgate rules and impose these rules on all. The result would be a moral order leading to peace and prosperity. From beginning to end the Hobbesian system depends on the idea of body—first on the natural bodies of men acting and reacting in much the same way as material bodies do, then on the great artificial body of the state constructed out of the powers obtained from the lesser bodies of men. All is matter or something acting very much like it. There is little or no place for inner awareness or consciousness in Hobbes's system.

Such thoroughgoing materialism was anathema to the Cambridge Platonists. To them, man's true being was something deeper and more fixed than the superficialities of bodily movement and the sensations resulting therefrom. Man's being, they insisted, contained a spiritual and intellectual core. Man, as body, might exist physically among his own kind in a physical landscape and react to sensations induced by matter, as Hobbes argued. But there is much more to man than that. He has an inner being. Experience can be received through the senses, but the more important kinds of experience are those purely of the mind. The Cambridge Platonists denied that principles of morality could be derived from a situation where men are acting and reacting merely as matter, a stuff which is dead, and which one can know only at second hand through the sometimes not too dependable signals from our senses. The difference between right and wrong can be known only by a living consciousness. Matter cannot presume to sit in judgment on other matter. Yet this is what the Cambridge Platonists felt that Hobbes was attempting to do.

The Cambridge Platonists lived in an age of growing materialism. Discoveries about the planetary system proved the intricate and astonishing character of the universe, and these discoveries overwhelmed many learned minds with the glories of the cosmic mechanism. Many thought that man and his institutions could be interpreted and explained in the light of these revelations. But the Cambridge Platonists opposed such a world view as a basis for a correct interpretation of man and his institutions. For them, the inner sensitivities of the mind far outweighed in importance those inspirations drawn from scientific discovery.

Richard Cumberland was drawn into this argument between Hobbes and the Cambridge Platonists. While generally sympathetic to the aims of the Platonists, he could not go along with their method of opposing Hobbes. Unlike the Cambridge Platonists he did not seek to discover standards of morality through ratiocination. He felt that moral standards are to be discovered largely through the senses as the individual absorbs and correctly interprets information about the character of the external world. But what Cumberland saw the individual taking in about this world was radically different from what Hobbes postulated. Instead of shifting the locus of argument to the plane of pure thought, as the Cambridge Platonists attempted to do, Cumberland claimed to stay in the here-and-now in order to face Hobbes on his own ground. But each interprets the terrain very differently. For Cumberland the self-interested actions of the individual were not, essentially, destructive but constructive. His purpose was to explain why this was so. With Cumberland we take an early, but incomplete, step in the direction of an idea that will eventually become an eighteenth-century commonplace, the idea that self-interest serves the public welfare.

Richard Cumberland was born in London in 1631. He attended Magdalene College at Cambridge, where he distinguished himself and where he was later elected fellow. While there, he began a lifelong friendship with Samuel Pepys, who in his famous diaries records his admiration and high respect for Cumberland's personal character and for his learning and scholarship. After graduation from Cambridge he entered the church and held positions as a country clergyman. In 1672 he published his major work, *De Legibus Naturae*. His deep concern about the attempts of James II to promote the Catholic religion caused him to react with a strong defense of Protestantism. This gained him favorable attention and, largely as a result, William III appointed him bishop of Peterborough in 1691. In later life he seriously studied ancient Jewish writings, although nothing was published from this work until after his death. He died in 1718 and was interred in his cathedral. Cumberland seems to have been a man of great simplicity combined with a seriousness of purpose. His holy duties were considerable and he carried them out with great devotion. Yet he found time for massive reading and deep scholarly investigation.

Cumberland's *De Legibus Naturae*, translated into English by John Maxwell and published by him under the title *A Treatise of the Laws of Nature* in 1727, is a long and involved work. It is difficult reading. The work is overrun with interminable modifying clauses which snag one's train of thought and cause one to back up again and again to gain Cumberland's meaning. Cumberland admits that the method of composing the work was not entirely satisfactory because it was "written by Starts at Intervals, such as an uncertain State of Health, and the weighty Cares of my holy Function, would permit."[2] According to Maxwell, in his preface to his translation, Cumberland had difficulties getting the book through the press. The manuscript was transcribed by an inexperienced hand, resulting in many errors, and the author, living in the country some distance from London, was not able to supervise closely the details of publication but left the task to a friend. To ease some of the difficulties in Cumberland's style, Maxwell says that he has tried to give a "helping hand" in his translation but without altering the sense of the work.

At the beginning of the *Treatise* Cumberland affirms that its "Face is not painted with the florid Colours of Rhetorick, nor are its Eyes sparkling and sportive, the Signs of a light Wit." To underline his seriousness of purpose he adds that the work "wholly applies it self, as it were, with the Composure and Sedateness of an old Man, to the Study of natural Knowledge, to gravity of Manners, and to the cultivation of severer Learning."[3] When Cumberland wrote this heavy warning to his readers he was less than forty-one years into a life that stretched to the age of eighty-seven.

Cumberland's immediate purpose in writing his *Treatise* was to reply to Hobbes, whose doctrines, he says, had "*so grossly perverted so many.*"[4] But he had in mind something more positive than merely a refutation of Hobbes.

He claims his larger purpose was to promote the public good by attempting to show how the conclusions of moral law are conveyed into and imprinted directly on the human mind from external sources. If he can accomplish this goal, he feels that he will have served mankind well.

The fundamental assumption underlying Cumberland's entire system is that moral law is derived from the laws of nature; that, underneath all, the foundations of moral law rest upon natural law. In order to know the moral laws governing the actions of men it is necessary, first of all, to understand the laws governing the world of matter. He is going to meet and oppose Hobbes on Hobbes's own ground.

Cumberland feels that the Platonists have not faced squarely the question of how the conclusions of moral law enter the mind, because they suppose the existence of "*innate Ideas,* as well [as] the Laws of Nature."[5] While the Platonists would agree that moral law must accord with natural law, they assume that external nature does not have to be consulted in order to reach moral conclusions. The mind is inherently capable of reaching these conclusions from its own resources. In short, moral ideas are born with us. For Cumberland such inner apprehensions of moral rules are not enough. He feels that relying on these apprehensions to reach moral law is too easy a way to deal with what is really a very complicated problem. Replying to the Platonists, he says, "I have not been so happy as to learn the Laws of Nature in so short a way."[6]

If one must understand nature in order to know man, then the problem, as Cumberland sees it, is to explain how this understanding is achieved, or as he puts it, how "the Powers of things, as well without as within us, conspire to *imprint* these Conclusions [of moral law] upon our Minds, and to give a *Sanction* to them."[7] Cumberland does not categorically deny that innate ideas exist, or that, if they do, they may in some way assist the individual in arriving at moral conclusions. But he feels, nevertheless, that the emphasis has been put in the wrong place, that it is more important to find out how external nature contributes to these conclusions.

Cumberland starts to answer this problem by saying that natural law is made known to us through our senses and by our daily experience. The first cause of all seen and felt effects of nature is the prime mover of nature, and this is God. We arrive, Cumberland says, "not at the *Knowledge of God* by immediate *Intuition* of his Perfections, but from his Effects first known by Sense and Experience."[8] Similarly, he argues, we must examine what we know about the world around us in order to understand the overreaching reality behind things, including the reality of moral law. He refuses to try an unassisted leap from mind all the way over to moral law. In his cautious way he insists on constructing a bridge between the two, a bridge of sense and experience to convey man gradually, but safely, over to his destination of a moral life. Cumberland looks upon his method as that of the empiricist, an investigator of facts and experience. He summarizes this point by saying that "Truths depend, not upon the *Will* of Men imposing and connecting Names arbitrarily, but upon the *Natures of Things* delineating their own Representations upon the Mind."[9]

But Cumberland insists there is an important and overriding consideration one must keep in mind when attempting to interpret the impressions received from nature, and this is that all things in nature are parts of a larger system and, as such, are intimately connected together. If one is to evaluate correctly the sense impressions received from the parts of nature, then one must be aware that the parts are bound together into a larger whole and that the properties of the parts are meaningful only in connection with this larger whole. Cumberland explains this important point in his philosophy as he says that "those Accidents of Bodies which are daily obvious to our Senses, such as the communication of Motion, Gravitation, the Actions of Light and Heat, Firmness and Fluidity, Rarefaction and Condensation, cannot be clearly explain'd, without having a respect to the whole material System, and to that Motion which is to be preserv'd therein." Developing this same point in the same place he adds that "no Effect of any Motion, connected with others, and Subordinate to them in a continued Series, can be exactly deduc'd, except all their Motions . . . be calculated and compar'd."[10] To understand parts one must understand the whole.

How might the pattern of operation of the parts of nature be described? The outstanding feature of the operation of Cumberland's "whole material System" might be described as one of reciprocation and accommodation. Parts move toward and then away from each other in a pattern of mutual adaptation and adjustment. "If we consider this *visible World*, with *Des Cartes* and others, as a most exquisite *Machine*," Cumberland writes, "we may perceive, that our Vortex is no otherwise daily preserv'd, than by *resisting* some *contrary Motions* of the neighboring Vortices . . . by a *circular Motion* of the Parts . . . and by causing its Parts to *yield to one another*."[11] He adds to this point by noting in another place that "the Motion of the corporeal World, dispersed thro' the several Parts thereof, is preserv'd by that mutual Communication, Cession, Acceleration, or Retardation, of all Motions."[12] Thus, he concludes, "the Motions of particular Bodies agree with the general Motion of the Whole, and are subservient thereto."[13] Cumberland's view of the world is one with parts moving in harmony with each other. It appears that his view was influenced by the discoveries of the new astronomers and by the pseudomechanical view that Descartes entertained about the nature of the universe. In this world there are no outright clashes of matter, no unexpected excursions of things. Everything operates smoothly, according to a plan. So, if we are to understand what our senses take in from the material world, we must be aware that our sense impressions come from a system that is coherent, not chaotic. The overriding character is one of design.

After establishing the physical world as an organized and predictable entity, Cumberland turns to his main task. This is to explain the rules of morality in light of our knowledge of this world. He relies heavily on the principle of design discovered in the world of matter to explain how moral law applies to the actions of men. He uses the principle of design because he feels that human life, being part of creation, cannot be separated from the greater patterns governing the universe. In fact, he seems to entertain the idea that the two worlds run together. To illustrate this belief, Cumberland enlarges the meaning of natural philosophy, or science, to include certain aspects of moral philosophy, as he explains that *"Natural Philosophy*, in the large Sense I now use it, does not only comprehend all those *Appearances of Natural Bodies*, which we know from Experiment, but also inquires into the Nature of our *Souls*."[14] It follows, then, if the principle of design is a key to understanding the natural world, it is also a principle useful in interpreting the moral world. Cumberland therefore concludes, in light of the design principle, "That the Connexion is no less necessary between human Action, however free . . . and their Effects, than between the Actions or Motions of mere Bodies, and the Effects thence demonstrated."[15] A determinate world for matter leads Cumberland into a determinate world for men.

Cumberland repeatedly emphasizes his belief in the sureness of the connection between cause and effect. He cannot bring himself to believe that actions, either material or human, can trail off into nothingness, disappearing without effect into a physical or social void. He frequently draws parallels from mathematics, arguing that social causes and their effects are no less sure than the steps in the connecting logic of geometry or algebra.[16] The underlying assumption supporting his belief that actions must run inevitably into effects is that the world contains a property of fullness, that it holds as much as one can conceive it to hold. He says that something like this "is observable in the Motions of the *Mundane* System, which arises from the Plenitude of the World, and the Contact of Bodies."[17] Cumberland sees bodies both in the material and social worlds existing in such close proximity that any movement of one body must be felt by others. Consequently, actions must always run into effects. But the impacts between bodies are, ultimately, not destructive ones. He goes on to explain that the powers of all individuals for self-defense are "so *pois'd*, that no one can be destroy'd by any other, to the hazard and damage of the Whole."[18] (We will return to this idea of plenitude or the fullness of nature later in this chapter because it is an important point for understanding Cumberland's system and also for appreciation of the work of some other writers we will take up later.)

If the social actions of man conform to a determinate pattern, how might this pattern be described? As we might expect, Cumberland finds the pattern to be one of reciprocation and accommodation. Drawing a parallel between the movements of human bodies and "all other *Bodies*," Cumberland describes how the social motion of the human body "is *propagated* far and wide, and does *not perish*, but *concurs* with other Motions to *perpetuate* the Successions of Things, or to preserve the Whole."[19] Just as the planets, for example, approach and give way to one another in their appointed rounds, in a pattern that results in the preservation of the solar system, so men in their social motions follow a pattern conducive to the preservation of society. If, at first glance, the immediate actions of men appear to have no larger purpose than the serving of self, a deeper appreciation of reality provided by the design principle makes us realize that the movements of the parts must have implications for the whole. With this in mind, we see that the actions of individuals assume larger or social implications. If matter acts in such a way as to preserve its collective integrity, Cumberland seems to ask, can anything less be expected of man?

So far in Cumberland's grand design of man and nature it appears that what is physical far outweighs in importance what is mental, that the operations of the mind are largely orchestrated by the operations of matter. It would appear that Cumberland is merely trying to replace Hobbes's destructive materialism with a kind of constructive materialism. But there is more to Cumberland's system than that. There are important voluntary aspects of man's character, and Cumberland sums them up under what he calls "benevolence," which he sees as the predominant motive behind men's actions. He gives no formal definition for this important motive and he seems not completely clear about its meaning. We can, however, discern a number of characteristics for benevolence from the many references he makes to the term. As one would expect, its meaning includes such things as kindness, generosity, charitable feelings, and a disposition to do good. At this point one might question Cumberland's reliance on such seemingly weak inclinations; kind thoughts would hardly seem sufficient to get the world's work done. John Maxwell, his translator, is also uneasy concerning Cumberland's possible intentions about these aspects of benevolence. He feels quite sure that the author of the *Treatise* did not mean the weakening kinds of benevolent feelings that might lead to the neglect of one's own welfare and the discouragement of industry.[20] Maxwell's point seems to be correct because Cumberland does include the strengthening motive of self-interest within his meaning for benevolence: "I suppose every one seeks *his own* Good, and that *to act in pursuit thereof*, adds to the *perfection* of his Nature."[21] He also says that a *"prudent* care of our own Happiness cannot be separated from the pursuit of the Happiness of others."[22] But Cumberland does not want to push the motive of self-interest too far because he feels that the "conduct of *Prudence*" should "either prevent or *root out* all *perverse* Self-love."[23] He cannot support an unlimited self-interest because this would sail too close to the doctrines of Hobbes. We would, therefore, conclude that Cumberland's meaning for benevolence includes self-interest but only in a moderate or controlled sense.

Cumberland also connects the motive of benevolence with the various activities of business. He includes, for example, those actions connected with "the *Exchange* of Things or *Services*,"[24] and what he calls "that less, but most useful, Benevolence, which is practis'd in all kinds of Agreements, Compacts, and Commerce, in which we either promise, or perform, any thing to others, under a Condition to be by them executed."[25] There are, therefore, economic and, perhaps, political motives among the several that Cumberland places under benevolence. It is easy to see how some of these motives could be connected with self-interest. Perhaps the best way to summarize Cumberland's understanding of benevolence is to include within it many, if not all, kinds of peaceful interaction among men. To Hobbes, human beings are destructive animals; to Cumberland, they are social beings.

We are now not far from a major conclusion drawn from Cumberland's grand design: personal and voluntary actions of the individual promote the public welfare. While we have already seen this conclusion by implication in Cumberland's discussion of certain actions connected with his motive of benevolence, there is more direct evidence of it available. Believing that both physical and moral law are controlled by a common underlying principle of design, Cumberland has to take only a small step to conclude that "human Actions, not unlike these [the coherent actions of matter], may be the no less proper Causes of preserving the whole System of Mankind, and making them happy."[26] Or, stating the same idea in another place, he says that "Motions of human bodies ever so little subject to the Determination and Direction of the human Will . . . when govern'd by the universal Benevolence of all rational Beings towards all, are the principal Causes of the publick Happiness of all."[27] And, carrying the same idea further, he refers to benevolence as a motive which, as he puts it, induces even those who carry on the mundane functions of life by the "Exchange of Things or Services" to benefit many others. It then follows, Cumberland continues, that "the *whole Happiness* . . . grows out of such *minute* offices of Humanity."[28] Clearly, the small and private actions of the individual for his own ends lead to the promotion and preservation of the public welfare.

Cumberland associates the concept of equilibrium with his conclusion that the "minute" actions of the individual are conducive to the public welfare. He describes how the "Parts and Powers of the System of the World" are so closely related "that there is nothing which may not give either Force or Opposition to any Body whatsoever, either now or hereafter. *This Complication* is yet more conspicuous in *Human Powers . . .* upon account of the additional Force, which the Powers of our *Mind* give to our *Bodily* Motions."[29] This potential for opposition is not destructive, however, because it is controlled by an "Equilibrium or Poize between the Parts of the whole System jointly consider'd, by which the whole System is preserv'd." More precisely, he describes how men enter into "Compacts" among themselves "by which their mutual Happiness may be both secur'd and increas'd." He then explains that "By *these Methods* the Powers of some will of necessity be counter poiz'd by others,"[30] and the actions of individuals will be brought into accord with the public welfare. We saw above how the condition of fullness or plenitude of the world works to limit actions, thus curbing their destructive potential. Added to this, we now have men using inner motives for voluntary agreements which achieve much the same result. It is interesting that Cumberland connects both of these conditions that restrict men's actions with ideas that are in essence physical—either the static condition of plenitude, which has to do with large numbers of bodies, or the dynamics of equilibrium, which is connected with movements toward a state of poise between bodies. His whole philosophy is saturated with ideas derived from nature, as was typical in his day.

But Cumberland does not have to rely entirely on parallels drawn from nature to prove that the actions of individuals are conducive to the public welfare. He also relies on a simple logic. Stating that the whole is nothing more than the sum of its parts, he goes on to say that the "Good of the Whole is nothing else but Good communicated to all the Parts." Consequently, "He . . . encreases the *common* Stock of Happiness, who benefits even *one*, without hurting any *other*."[31] But how, specifically, is the welfare of the individual to be actually increased? At the beginning of the *Treatise* Cumberland brings up what he calls "*Propositions of Unchangeable Truth, Which direct our voluntary Actions.*"[32] These propositions precede all civil law and government. One of them is what he refers to as a "*Division* of Things, and of human Services."[33] What he means is a division of goods and services so that each individual has some adequate and reasonable share. The welfare of the individual depends upon his having such a share. It follows, Cumberland continues, if the "Preservation of a *Whole*, consisting of mutually *divided Parts*, (such as Mankind is,) consists in the Preservation of the *divided Parts*," then the "Preservation of the *divided* Parts, that is, of particular Men, requires the *divided* use of Things and of human Labour."[34] As a practical support to this argument, he adds later that this division is also necessary because "it is *impossible*, That the same thing, or the Labour of the same Man, can serve the contrary Wills of many Men."[35] Individual actions to secure an adequate supply of material necessities are a necessary part of Cumberland's conception of the public welfare. These actions are justified as part of his proof that the good of the whole consists of the sum of benefits enjoyed by the parts. Again we see that self-interest, this time directly connected with property rights, is part of moral law.

Cumberland's attitude toward property rights, we should add, is essentially moderate. He does not support any program for economic leveling or material equality. On the other hand he does not countenance unbridled accumulation of personal wealth. He states clearly that in providing for one's own material welfare we must always "Abstain from invading another's Property, and take care, That we promote the Publick Good. This limited self-love displays it-self chiefly in *Temperance, Frugality* and *Modesty*."[36] Cumberland's aim in supporting property rights is the rather limited one of making secure for the individual enough goods and services to preserve his own welfare. Anything less reduces the public welfare and goes against the ultimate purpose of his whole philosophical system which is, as he often puts it, "the public Happiness." Cumberland does not go into practical details of how property rights of the individual are to be achieved and maintained. His purpose is to illustrate their philosophical necessity rather than to explain actual procedures on how to obtain and preserve them. The *Treatise* is anything but a handbook on procedures of public administration.

As we saw earlier, Cumberland's system stands on the principle of design. This principle is fundamental to his work and to the work of other writers we will take up later. At this point we will explore some of the ideas behind the principle. This will help to provide insights into Cumberland's system and those of these other writers. The best single discussion about the principle of design can be found in that most impressive work by Arthur Lovejoy, *The Great Chain of Being* (1936).

Lovejoy's primary purpose is to trace the genesis of the idea of the "Great Chain of Being," the metaphysical belief that the underlying structure of the universe, both material and social, might be explained in terms of a cosmic hierarchy rising through imperceptible steps from the simplest to the most complex of existences. This was one of the common themes in Western thought during the seventeenth and eighteenth centuries and references to it can be found in many of the works of leading minds in science, philosophy, theology, and poetry. It colors the entire imagination of its age.

The design principle is closely connected with a key idea underlying the chain of being, an idea Lovejoy calls the "principle of plenitude."[37] Going back into the classics, he discusses the evolution of the concept of pure ideas or essences in the works of Plato. He then shows that these pure ideas or essences in the Platonic philosophy were meant to have connections with and implications for the real or material world. Lovejoy then discusses the reasoning that justified this projection of ideas into the world of matter. If the world of ideas is full of all kinds of things, and it is, then reality must, it was argued, be a "complete translation of all the ideal possibilities into actuality," or the created world must be an "exhaustive replica" of the contents of the other world.[38] If the real world was meant to reflect, in any degree, the contents of the world of ideas, then it was meant to do so fully and completely. If not, then the relationship between the two worlds would be left to hazard and fortuitous circumstance. The character of the cosmos would then be arbitrary and unpredictable, a thought alien to Plato's philosophy. Lovejoy calls this "strange and pregnant theorem of 'fullness', of the realization of conceptual possibility in actuality,"[39] the principle of plenitude.

The principle of design can be seen as a logical extension of the idea of plenitude. The very act of creation, which underlies the condition of plenitude, implies organization, and the end-products of creation must reflect this permeating property of organization. As Lovejoy explains, the "principle of plenitude had latent in it a sort of absolute cosmical determinism." There is "no room for any contingency anywhere in the universe."[40] Cumberland, as we have seen, subscribes to the idea of plenitude, so it is not at all surprising to see his heavy dependence on the principle of design. One logically runs into the other.

One other implication of the principle of plenitude should be mentioned because, again, we see it in Cumberland and in the work of our later writers. This is the idea that nature has a property of continuousness. If the created world has to be as full as it possibly can be, then there cannot be any gaps or holes in creation. If there is space for an intermediate type between existing types then the type must be realized. Lovejoy mentions the horror that Leibniz felt in imagining vacant spaces in the fabric of nature. Such hiatuses force the mind into unbelievable contortions in attempting to explain and understand the phenomena of nature.[41] Nothingness is much harder to explain than somethingness. If all creation is shaped by a continuity of its parts, by a smooth blending of neighboring types into one another, then one would be struck by the property of wholeness implicit in all the parts. Nothing stands apart from the whole. This vision of the massive integrity of the world greatly impressed Pascal, who wrote, "it is impossible to know the parts without knowing the whole or the whole without knowing all the parts."[42] We have already discussed Cumberland's dependence on this idea. Again, it appears to be derived from the principle of plenitude.

Lovejoy emphasizes the importance of the principle of plenitude, and its corollaries of design and continuity, in shaping educated opinion about the structure of the universe during the two centuries after Copernicus. It was, for example, not so much the observational discoveries by astronomers that gave impetus to the new cosmography, Lovejoy argues, but, rather, the deep yearning to discover the underlying design which must be inherent in all of creation. Kepler's discoveries about planetary motion were inspired more by a desire to find a rational plan, an order in the heavens, than by knowledge he gained by consulting existing records of planetary movements. "The more important features of the new conception of the world," Lovejoy writes, "owed little to any new hypotheses based upon the sort of observational grounds which we should nowadays call 'scientific.' They were chiefly derivative from philosophical and theological premises. They were, in short, manifest corollaries of the principle of plenitude."[43] If the principle of plenitude had such an importance influence in shaping educated thought about scientific matters, is it not likely that it also had an important effect on patterns of thought in social theory and moral philosophy? If we keep Cumberland in mind, the answer is, clearly, yes.

Cumberland is a pivotal figure in our history of the idea of self-interest and the public welfare. With him, we see an early attempt to prove in philosophical terms that the voluntary acts of the individual are an integral part of the collective welfare. And, what is important, he recognizes self-interest as one of the motives behind these acts. But we have not, as yet, reached the conclusion that self-interest is the dominant act leading to the public welfare, because Cumberland's many and varied actions of the individual, motivated by "benevolence," can hardly be reduced to the single motive of self-interest. Under Cumberland's notion of benevolence one can find acts leading to personal gain or, in other words, acts done through self-interest. But many other actions under benevolence have other objectives. Cumberland shows some awareness of the fact that actions done through self-interest ultimately help to serve the public welfare. As the individual fulfills contractual obligations with others, while pursuing benefits for himself, he serves not only his own material needs but those of many others. But Cumberland devotes more attention to acts serving the welfare of others in a direct way, acts of benevolence from disinterested motives. Acts of kindness and generosity, for example, serve the needs of others and, at the same time, evoke similar acts in return. As a result the public happiness is served on a large scale, and served directly. Self-interest is a part of Cumberland's general motive of benevolence but only a limited part.

There is a vast difference between the accounts given by Cumberland and by our final writer, Adam Smith, about the relationship between self-interest and the public welfare. Cumberland's motive of benevolence leads the individual through many kinds of interactions with others, but, clearly, benevolence is not to be confused with the motive inspiring the participants in Smith's market system. Cumberland discusses the formal character of "compacts," in which one party agrees to give something on condition of receiving something else in return, but this can hardly be reduced to the pressured haggling and bargaining between buyer and seller which is so necessary for the proper functioning of Smith's market system. And Cumberland uses the idea of equilibrium to describe his ideal of a balanced relationship between various members of society, but this can hardly be reduced to Smith's conception of an economic equilibrium, which is an ideal of his market system. In spite of the wide disparities among the ideas of these two great minds, we will see how certain of Cumberland's ideas are slowly transformed by later thinkers so that, eventually, the ideas will serve as prototypes even for the speculations of Smith.[44] Certain ideas of Cumberland will be reshaped, relocated, and then be refilled with a new and more substantial content—a content appealing more to the empirically minded eighteenth century. If we examine this process closely enough, perhaps we will be able to discern the invisible hand of Cumberland having an influence on the operations.

5

Shaftesbury and Butler
The Psychology of Self-Interest
and the Public Welfare

> The balance of Europe, of Trade, or power, is strictly
> sought after; while few have heard of the balance of their
> passions.
>
> Shaftesbury

Man's emergence into the modern world had not been an easy one.
Hobbes had forced him to run the deadly gauntlet of his own passions
and, even if he survived and eventually conquered his passions, he still
had to live under the bonds of absolute authority. But, as we have just
seen, help was being made available to modern man. Despite Hobbes's
claims to the contrary, perhaps nature had not been so hard and unrelenting when designing man's soul. To Cumberland, man's inner nature
could not be the only place in an otherwise organized universe where
utter capriciousness reigned. Every part of nature was a product of
design, and so must be the soul of modern man. And, more than that,
Cumberland saw that man enjoyed powers that made him his own agent.
These powers produced in man a cooperative and accommodating character causing him to go along rather than go against. There was now the
distinct possibility that man could look to his own passions to find a gauge
to measure his social self, rather than having to resort to the cold and
remote processes of reason for this purpose. But it was still too early to
accept such an idea as a philosophical truth. Alexander Pope had not as
yet confidently announced that "The proper study of Mankind is man."
There remained considerable work to be done and many minds to be
convinced before such a bold opinion could receive wide support.

   In this chapter we will examine the works of two writers who advanced
and consolidated certain of Cumberland's insights about self-interest.
They are Anthony Ashley Cooper, third earl of Shaftesbury, and Joseph
Butler. We will also mention Alexander Pope because his poetry dramati-
cally summarizes the influence of Shaftesbury and Butler on educated
minds of the early eighteenth century.

   With the writings of Shaftesbury, the position of man improves greatly.
Shaftesbury's thoughts about the nature of man rise upward into the
light. His works project a sense of confidence and understanding about
the soul of man. The key inspiration propelling Shaftesbury's thoughts is
an intensely positive, even lyrical, feeling for nature. Earlier writers, awed

by the immensity and complexity of nature, had dared, occasionally, to express their wonder and admiration for creation. But Shaftesbury's reaction to nature runs into an unbridled enthusiasm. A complete faith and trust in creation spills over into his interpretation of the character of man, as he gathers from nature a profound respect for man's character and its position in the scheme of creation. Man emerges from the works of Shaftesbury as complete unto himself, containing all that is necessary for attaining the moral life. Creation was designed with a space fit for man to occupy and Shaftesbury sees in man all of the necessary qualities for him to occupy this space in a proper manner. With Shaftesbury, man's lack of righteousness recedes into the background to be replaced by properties of rightness. He was, indeed, a friend to man.

Shaftesbury was born in London in 1671. His grandfather, the first earl and a leading political figure of his day, employed John Locke as a secretary. Locke was given supervision of young Shaftesbury's education. At an early age Shaftesbury acquired a knowledge of Greek and Latin which laid the groundwork for the great admiration he showed for classical writers in his later life. He traveled in Europe and, especially, in Italy, where he studied paintings, sculpture, and music. After returning to England he continued his studies and, some years later, decided to seek political office, becoming a member of the House of Commons in 1695. Due to poor health and a probable disenchantment with politics, he left the Commons in 1698. He married in 1709 but, because of worsening health, he returned with his wife to Italy for the milder climate in 1711. He died in Naples in 1713.

Shaftesbury's major works were collected and published in 1711 under the title *Characteristics of Men, Manners, Opinions, Times*, which went through eleven editions by 1790. This work exercised a major influence on moral philosophy during the eighteenth century. Shaftesbury is usually seen as the founder of the moral sense theory, a belief that the character of man contains an innate sense which enables him to distinguish right from wrong, although anticipations of such a theory can be found earlier in the works of the Cambridge Platonists. As with the Cambridge men and Cumberland, Shaftesbury is critical of the doctrines of Hobbes, although he seems to indicate that these doctrines were no great threat because, as he puts it, "Mr. Hobbes's character and base slavish principles in government took off the poison of his philosophy."[1] The ideas of Locke were a more serious threat. As much as he respected his old tutor, Shaftesbury felt that Locke's attack on innate ideas "struck at all fundamentals, threw all order and virtue out of the world, and made the very ideas of [order and virtue] . . . *unnatural*, and without foundation in our minds."[2] "Thus virtue, according to Mr. Locke," Shaftesbury claims, "has no other measure, law, or rule, than fashion and custom."[3]

51

According to Shaftesbury, Locke "wanted a law for fashion and opinion. .. . As if to the Italian or other good masters . . . he had said that the *law of harmony was opinion. . . .* Had Mr. Locke been a *virtuoso*, he would not have philosophized thus."[4] Shaftesbury strongly opposed the ethical relativism of Hobbes and Locke. He was out to illustrate that there are points in ethics which are fixed and unchangeable, and with the help of knowledge gained from nature he will find them intrinsic to the soul of man.

To Shaftesbury, moral philosophy has fallen on bad days. Its scholarly practitioners have "immured her, poor lady, in colleges and cells, and have set her servilely to such works as those in the mines."[5] Moral philosophy no longer sees the light of the common world and no longer makes itself available to instruct statesmen as it did in ancient times. Shaftesbury wants to bring the subject back into the open, into discussions and conversations among cultivated and liberally educated minds. In order to understand mankind, Shaftesbury argues, "'tis necessary to study man in particular, and know the creature as he is in himself."[6] And this is best accomplished far away from the builders of systems, whose method "to prevent good sense is to set up something in the room of it."[7] A mind enjoying a broad range of interests, one that is sensitive to many things, is to Shaftesbury a mind of good sense. It is a mind formed "from that excellent school which we call the world" and it "is a better guide to judgement than improved sophistry and pedantic learning."[8] A gentleman of learning with artistic interests is a better judge of the nature of man than the insular mind concentrating on the profundities of systems. Shaftesbury says, however, that the study of moral philosophy is not for every one. It is for those who, if they have not been everywhere and studied everything, have, at least, a serious appreciation of the worlds of literature and the arts. So Shaftesbury chooses to write in a style he feels would be attractive to such minds. Such a style would appeal to members of an intelligent leisure class. It would avoid narrow paths of logic inevitably leading to cold conclusions. It would depend on literary skills of allusion and example to introduce ideas gradually, by attractive means, into the mind of his reader. Unlike Cumberland, he does not feel it necessary at the beginning to warn his reader of the heavy going that lies ahead. He assumes that his familiar and lively method of expression will attract his reader's interest and understanding. And, usually, he is right.

The central point in Shaftesbury's work is an idea we have already encountered. It is the design principle. He refers repeatedly to this principle throughout his works, expressing it more completely and more vividly than previous writers. As we have seen, it rests on the assumption of an ordered universe. The forces of all creation operate according to a regular and dependable pattern. There is no place for chance or accident in the structure of nature. Everything follows a course imposed by the

laws of nature. For example, Shaftesbury discusses a "designing principle" in the "economy or government of the universe."[9] In another place
he implies design as he refers to "that economy to which all things are
subservient."[10] Rising to the highest conceivable level in creation, he
identifies the prime mover of all things as the "wise economist, and
powerful chief, whom all the elements and powers of Nature serve!"[11]
Descending to inferior levels, he describes how, in the structure of each
plant and animal body, each organ fulfills a purpose in the overall function of the body, as he says, "All things in this world are united."[12]
Shaftesbury, seemingly, is overwhelmed with the thought of "the mutual
dependency of things! . . . the order, union, and coherence of the
whole!"[13] Design runs through the parts and throughout the whole.
Nothing exists apart; everything is connected within itself and with the
whole.

To Shaftesbury the order and harmony inherent in the universe make
it an "exquisite system of self-governed matter."[14] He admires the universe, as would an artist, for its fine balance and proportion. He sees in it a
beauty that saturates the senses, and his intense admiration converts him
into an evangelist about the wonders of nature. Shaftesbury's appeal to
his readers is not so much to their reason as to their unconscious predilec-
tions, to their sense of beauty, worth, and rightness. Such an appeal made
a strong impression, and he, more than any other writer, helped to make
nature and the design principle a familiar concept in the mind of the
eighteenth century.

After pointing out the property of design throughout the length and
breadth of creation, Shaftesbury then turns to his study of man and,
especially, to man's mental constitution. This is important because a study
of man's inner drives and affections is, according to Shaftesbury, "the
philosophy which by Nature has the preeminence above all other science
or knowledge."[15] But this study of inner man, he makes clear, is not to be
confused with Locke's epistemology. It is not concerned with such questions as "how [do] I come by my ideas . . . which are simple, and which
complex?" It is not concerned with "knowing how I form or compound
those ideas which are marked by words." Rather, and much more important, it is the study of questions such as "a right idea of life," of "how I
come by . . . an opinion of worth and virtue."[16] Shaftesbury is not concerned with the means by which the mind acquires and processes ideas
but with the ends existing in the mind by which it distinguishes between
what is worthy and what is unworthy. In short, it is a question of how the
mind judges values rather than how it processes its impressions.

Shaftesbury finds that the mind contains numerous drives and affections. Replying to Hobbes and others who would reduce everything to the
drive of self-interest, to those who would transform all public affections,

such as "civility, hospitality, humanity toward strangers or people in distress"[17] into self-love in another guise, Shaftesbury says that the mind also contains "passion, humour, caprice, zeal, faction, and a thousand other springs, which are counter to self-interest."[18] The more important question, he maintains, is whether a person pursues his self-interest in the right way or not. "The question would not be, 'who loved himself, or who not,' but 'who loved and served himself the rightest, and after the truest manner.'"[19] Shaftesbury will not be drawn into arguing whether certain human feelings, nominally denominated as social, are really inverted forms of self-love. He transfers arguments about self-love over to his own ground by insisting that the more important question is whether self-interested feelings are worthy or not. His answer to this question depends upon whether self-interest is consistent with the public good or not. If it is consistent with the public good, it is a good affection; if not, then it is a bad one. "Thus the affection towards self-good may be a good affection or an ill one."[20] Shaftesbury feels that the proper study of self-interest is not the quantity people have of it but its quality. Again, the emphasis is on values.

Self-interest is an innate motive in man. "We know," Shaftesbury says, "that every creature has a private good and interest of his own, which Nature has compelled him to seek."[21] But man also has another main motive in his constitution and it is as natural as self-interest. This is a sense of public good or welfare. "If eating and drinking be natural," he says, "herding is so too. If any appetite or sense be natural, the sense of fellowship is the same."[22] Shaftesbury admits, however, that "Universal good, or the interest of the world in general, is a kind of remote philosophical subject. That greater community falls not easily under the eye." Nevertheless, "All men have naturally their share of the combining principle."[23] To Shaftesbury, all of the numerous drives and affections in man come under these two headings—interest in self and interest in the public. (It should be noted that he does mention one other category, the "unnatural affections" which lead neither to private nor public good. But these need not concern us here.)

Shaftesbury says that private and public interests are served and controlled by "a due balance and counterpoise in the affections."[24] This condition of equilibrium is the result of the design principle penetrating the soul of man. He explains this point with the aid of an analogy. He says the balance in the "inward anatomy" of the mind is not unlike that balance existing among the organs making up the real anatomy. "'Tis certain that the order or symmetry of this inward part is in itself no less real and exact than that of the body."[25] Design dominates the physical anatomy and so it must the mind of man. Moving to another analogy, this time connected with a stringed musical instrument, he describes how each string is drawn up to just the proper tension when the instrument is put into proper tonal balance. Similarly, he concludes that each chord in the human spirit is precisely adjusted so as to achieve a balance of the soul. Shaftesbury refers to this condition as the "tuning of the passions."[26] This system or inner organization he calls the "economy of the passions"[27] and, in this "united structure and fabric of the mind," he describes how there exists a "necessary connection and balance of the affections."[28] No one motive in the mind is designed to dominate any other. There is a harmonious balance among all the elements, both those serving private interest and those serving the public welfare. Shaftesbury, therefore, concludes from this condition, as imposed on the soul by the principle of design, "That to be well affected towards the public interest and one's own is not only consistent but inseparable."[29] Design penetrates all, including the human soul. It creates a harmony within the human mind and, while doing so, causes the actions of the individual to accord with society.

Shaftesbury has described the balanced structure of the mind and, in doing so, concludes that self-interest necessarily goes along with interest in the public welfare, but he does not define his state of balance in the mind with great precision. Given the determinant structure of the mind, he indicates that what goes on in the mind might be explained in terms of a "scheme of moral arithmetic."[30] But at the same time he seems aware that the passions and affections are not literally things that can be measured and treated with a high degree of exactness. His work on the mind emphasizes the qualitative and relational, but, nevertheless, he glances toward the possibility of their being studied in some quantitative way.

Shaftesbury comes closest to describing the precise conditions of his state of mental balance as he explains why the individual is obliged to maintain this state of balance. Taking up the social affections, he argues that, if they are not adequately exercised, the individual will become morose and miserable. Man is a creature whose dependence on social life is great. If he becomes indolent and indifferent to the concerns of society, "the passions thus restrained will force their prison," break out, and assume unnatural forms which will destroy "all inward order and economy" of the mind.[31] Repressed emotions will out, and will do so in vicious forms. On the other hand, Shaftesbury is aware that social passions may become too strong and that this might lead to the individual neglecting his own welfare. This is as bad as their being too weak.

In the case of the affections serving the self, the greatest potential problem, Shaftesbury feels, is that, because they are the "home affections," they will become too strong. He then gives several examples. The desire and love for one's own life may become obsessive so that, eventually, it will degenerate into fear. Anger, while necessary occasionally to protect the individual, may mount into mischief and possibly into self-destruction. Or pleasure may overextend itself into indulgent and licentious behavior. And the drive for wealth, being carried too far, may shrink the individual into covetousness. Consequently, the individual is obliged to avoid extremes in his passions and affections. Not to do so leads to a life of mental pain and, possibly, physical misery. Man is so constructed by nature that he is made for the "pursuit of happiness,"[32] a term that Shaftesbury seems to have borrowed from Cumberland, and the most effective way to pursue happiness is to preserve the balance which nature has provided for the motives in the mind.

Shaftesbury emphasizes the completeness of internal man. Each of his motives, whether private or social, is treated as a distinct entity, yet each is part of larger and unified whole, the soul of the individual. Compared to those who propose to "new-frame the human heart . . . to reduce all its motions, balances, and weights, to that one principle and foundation of a cool and deliberate selfishness,"[33] Shaftesbury insists on a comprehensive and balanced view of inner man. He sees man as also made up of motives arising from social impulses. But in replying to those who reduce all motives to self-interest, Shaftesbury will not bend the human soul too far in the opposite direction. He would not make man into a self-denying saint because man, being by nature what he is, must have sufficient inner room for motives serving his own immediate interests. He cannot live on the consideration of others alone. Thus self-interest is a necessary component in what Shaftesbury calls man's "moral kind of architecture."[34] Self-interest exists alongside motives of a social nature, and all are necessary in the overall structure of the character given to man by nature. As a result self-interest must be involved with social interest. One cannot be cut off from the other because they are both integral parts of the whole. Man is a complex equation but one containing a certain design. If the individual puts too high or low a value on certain points in the equation and the solution comes out wrong, the blame does not rest with the equation. It rests with the individual.

Shaftesbury's work, as we have seen, is put mainly in terms of philosophical psychology. He explores inner man in the context of the principle of design. There is very little in his work that can be specifically called economic. While it is true that his important motive of self-interest can have considerable influence on economic matters, as the individual strives for material gain, Shaftesbury focuses his attention in other directions. But there is one clue in his work pointing toward the kind of economic policy he probably preferred, and it is buried in a remark on a subject having nothing to do with economics. Shaftesbury advocated a large degree of freedom for the individual in making decisions about moral questions. He felt that the individual was properly equipped by nature to deal with such decisions. He also carries this advocacy of individual freedom over into the criticism of ideas, arguing that wit and humor may often penetrate to the true meaning of things if they are not put down by pedantry or heavy pronouncements from established authority. But if wit is used too freely, might it not grow into "scurrilous buffoonery"? Shaftesbury, answering his own question, thinks not, and it is in his answer that we see the clue to his economic policy. He says, "wit is its own remedy. Liberty and commerce bring it to its true standard. The only danger is, the laying an embargo. The same thing happens here, as in the case of trade. Impositions and restrictions reduce it to a low ebb. Nothing is so advantageous to it as a free port."[35] A strong and vigorous give-and-take in ideas is as beneficial as a strong and vigorous competition in economic life. Each brings things to their true level. This is hardly sufficient evidence to induct Shaftesbury into the camp of free traders, a group having very few members in his day. His seeming inclination toward free trade probably was a carry-over from his desire for freedom of the individual to make moral decisions rather than from any detailed study of economic life. But this is a possible example of how philosophical belief may influence economic ideas.

Shaftesbury's most important contribution to the philosophical discussion of the eighteenth century was his resolution of the problem of private interest and the public welfare. He brought this problem into the forefront of philosophical discussion and he dealt with it in such a way that it drew interested reactions in the conversations of opinion-makers and in the works of widely read authors. The problem was no longer buried in the repellent thoughts of Hobbes or under the complex layers of prose of the Cambridge men and Cumberland. It became the common property of many. Shaftesbury was no popularizer but his work did have a much broader appeal than that of previous writers, who had argued the problem in such unattractive or involved ways. Shaftesbury's method of bringing together into peaceful and necessary cooperation the two major drives in man proved appealing and convincing to many.

Shaftesbury emphasized the necessary balance between inner concerns of self-interest and social welfare. Joseph Butler, our next writer, takes this conclusion and explores it in more detail. Shaftesbury treated interests in self and society as essentially two separate powers in the mind, running in tandem, pulling the individual toward a life of virtue. Butler finds that the two motives not only work in a coordinate manner but that each blends largely into the other. He finds that a proper self-love is indivisible from an interest in the social welfare, and he makes his point in a clear and direct way. In doing this he advances considerably Shaftesbury's pioneering work on the inherent harmony between motives of self-interest and of the public welfare.

Joseph Butler was born in 1692 in Wantage, Berkshire, the son of a wealthy draper. His father planned that he should enter the Presbyterian church but young Butler, after considerable thought, decided to enter the Church of England. He was admitted to Oriel College, Oxford, in 1715 to study for the ministry. After entering the church, he moved through a number of positions and, eventually, was elected bishop of Bristol, later becoming bishop of Durham. His two major works are the *Sermons* (1726) and the *Analogy of Religion* (1736). Butler was not much interested in the realities of church politics, being preoccupied for long periods with the study of abstract ideas. He did, however, place emphasis on the formalities of church attendance and external observances of the Christian religion. He died in 1752 and was buried in Bristol cathedral.

At the beginning of the *Sermons* Butler says that morals can be treated either in terms of "the abstract relations of things," a method which lends itself to "the most direct and formal proof," or in terms "of fact," a method which deals with "what the particular nature of man is, its several parts, their economy or constitution." This second method, Butler feels, is better "adapted to satisfy a fair mind; and is more easily applicable to the several particular relations and circumstances in life."[36] This is the method he plans to follow in his investigations. It is clear that Cumberland, Shaftesbury, and now Butler all felt that their approaches to moral philosophy were superior to the more deductive approaches of, say, the Cambridge Platonists. They placed their emphasis on man and his normal motives and activities. But it is also evident that what they considered to be a more "realistic" approach to man was still considerably colored by abstraction.

Following both Cumberland and Shaftesbury, Butler bases his system on the principle of design. He repeats arguments similar to theirs in describing how design permeates everything in the universe, how everything from the highest to the lowest is intricately contrived and, at the same time, organized into a magnificent plan. His acceptance of the design principle rests, like Shaftesbury's, on a rather simple and straightforward use of analogy. He says there is, obviously, close integration among the parts of the human body to serve the physical ends of human life; so, similarly, there must exist a parallel kind of organization of the elements in the human mind to serve the moral ends of man. He argues that, just as eyes were given to see with, so, for example, a sense of shame was implanted by nature in the mind in order to prevent shameful actions.[37] Each human motive has a necessary function in the "inward frame" of man, and by studying these motives we can "get the idea of the system or constitution of human nature."[38]

Following Shaftesbury quite closely, Butler says natural human motives fall into two categories, one "respecting self, and tending to private good," and the other respecting "society, and tending to promote public good, the happiness of that society."[39] But then he deviates from Shaftesbury's lead when he says that both categories of motives come under the control and supervision of a third, which he calls "conscience." This supreme inner power Butler describes as a "principle of reflection" which sits in judgment on a person's "heart, temper, and actions."[40] Butler criticizes Shaftesbury for not placing enough emphasis on conscience in his conception of human nature. He feels that Shaftesbury left too great a degree of freedom to passion and that, as a result, the individual might at times be tempted to exceed the bounds of virtue. Shaftesbury helped to free man from the weight of Hobbes's absolute authority, but he has, perhaps, gone too far in the direction of freedom. Butler feels that man's character was not made for him "to act at random, and live at large up to the extent of his natural power, as passion, humour, wilfulness, happen to carry him." Instead man is equipped with a power to control himself, or "*he is in the strictest and most proper sense a law to himself*. He hath the rule of right within."[41] Shaftesbury pointed strongly toward man's being a complete moral entity in himself. Butler reinforces this point by adding the power of conscience as a guarantor of man's moral behavior.

With the principle of conscience in mind, Butler takes up the motive of self-love. He says that those who would see the hidden hand of self-love behind every benevolent act are wrong. "Everything is what it is, and not another thing," he replies.[42] Like Shaftesbury he insists that the important question is whether the act fits the *whole* character of man, whether it "becomes such creatures as we are."[43] Whether an act is interested or disinterested is of secondary importance compared to the question of whether it is appropriate or inappropriate to the character given to man by nature. Genuine acts of self-interest accord with the natural structure of man's emotions and, especially, with the supervisory motive of conscience. But these acts must be cool, reasonable, and intelligent. When they are, they then accord with both categories of the human constitution, the self and the social.

After civilizing the drive of self-love by placing it under the tutelage of conscience, Butler concludes that self-interest and social interest are inherently harmonious motives. "These ends," he says, "do indeed perfectly coincide; and to aim at public and private good are so far from being inconsistent, that they mutually promote each other."[44] "Self-love in its due degree is as just and morally good, as any affection whatever."[45] In fact Butler goes so far as to say that the world is in need of more people who cultivate and promote their own good or interest. He says, "self-love is one chief security of our right behaviour towards society."[46] Butler's great confidence in the social efficacy of self-love is best shown when, at one point, he separates the personal intentions of the agent during acts of self-interest from the larger social effects of these acts. Just as a person preserves himself by acting from the base appetite of hunger, without any reasoned consideration about the desirability of life, so "by acting merely from regard (suppose) to reputation, without any consideration of the good of others, men often contribute to public good. In both these instances . . . [men] carry on ends, the preservation of the individual and good of society, which they themselves have not in their view or intention."[47] The individual, in his private acts, is an unknowing tool of nature in furthering the greater ends of society. In this statement Butler clearly anticipates Adam Smith's famous invocation of the "invisible hand."

Butler, in order to strengthen his point that interests in self and in society are inherently harmonious, replies to those who argue that such interests are unalterably opposed. Their arguments, he says, claim that one interest is opposed to the other because the more one devotes his time or wealth to serving society the less he has remaining to serve his own interests. More time or wealth for one interest means less for the other. The fallacy of such arguments, Butler says, lies in the confusing of quantities of time or wealth with personal happiness. As one devotes more of his time or wealth to the ends of society, Butler counters, it is still very possible to experience greater personal happiness, the latter obviously being connected with self-interest. The false reasonings about this point, Butler says, "arise from our notions of property. . . . People are so very much taken up with one subject [property], that they seem from it to have formed a general way of thinking, which they apply to other things that they have nothing to do with."[48] States of mind, one category, cannot be measured in terms appropriate to such things as time and wealth, which are other categories. Butler feels that he has proved "that there is no peculiar rivalship or competition between self-love and benevolence."[49]

The works of Shaftesbury and Butler on the problem of self-interest and the public welfare greatly impressed many literary minds of the early eighteenth century. This problem became a leading one for writers on the subject of ethics. The most famous literary figure attracted to the problem of self-interest was Alexander Pope (1688–1744), probably the most widely read author in Britain and America at the time. Critics have emphasized how Pope's work reflects with great fidelity the leading intellectual problems of his day. In the most popular poem, *An Essay on Man*, completed in 1734, Pope addresses the question of self-interest and the social welfare, and we see the influence of Shaftesbury and Butler at work.

Pope devotes the opening section of the *Essay* to the principle of design. The purpose is to set the principle in the foreground in order to understand better what Pope calls "this scene of Man," which he sees as "A mighty maze! but not without a plan."[50] If we can understand the pattern underlying creation, Pope says, this "May tell why Heav'n has made us as we are."[51] One feature that Pope sees running throughout all of nature is that of violent change, as evidenced by earthquakes, storms, and droughts. Yet he also recognizes the existence of a background of order against which these events take place. If nature contains volatile elements, can we expect anything different for man? Pope answers, clearly, that we cannot. He explains:

> Better for Us, perhaps, it might appear,
> Were there all harmony, all virtue here;
> That never air or ocean felt the wind;
> That never passion discompos'd the mind.
> But ALL subsists by elemental strife;
> And Passions are the elements of Life.
> The gen'ral ORDER, since the whole began,
> Is kept in Nature, and is kept in Man.[52]

The passions are the counterpart in man of the volatile elements in nature, and, while very powerful, they are subject to order just as those in nature are. How are we to discover the character of this order? Pope looks to Newton's method for an answer: "Could he whose rules the rapid Comet bind,/ Describe or fix one movement of his Mind?"[53] Pope thinks not. Reason alone is not sufficient to understand the passions.

> Alas what wonder! Man's superior part
> Uncheck'd may rise, and climb from art to art;
> But when his own great work is but begun,
> What Reason weaves, by Passion is undone.[54]

In spite of his emphasis on the passions, Pope still sees reason as an important part of the character of man. It is the counterpart in man of the underlying order in nature. He then summarizes human equivalents of the principles of change and of order in nature. They are: "Self-love, to urge, and Reason, to restrain."[55] Man, like nature, is composed of two elements, one for action and one for order.

Pope then describes the relationships between self-love and reason as he says: "Self-love, the spring of motion, acts the soul;/ Reason's comparing balance rules the whole."[56] Self-love is the animating force behind the passions and, Pope adds, like the active force of gravity in the physical world, its power becomes greater as the object of its attention grows nearer. Then Pope brings the element of order into his general description of the interaction of the two principles in man. Despite the seeming anarchy of the passions he sees an order ultimately coming out of this strife: "Passions, like Elements, tho' born to fight,/ Yet, mix'd and soften'd, in his [God's] work unite."[57] Reason is the bringer of order as it mixes the passions and, in doing so, curbs their more violent properties and introduces a harmony into their seeming disorder.

After this very general description of the internal results of the interaction between self-love and reason, Pope then goes into a detailed discussion of man as a social being. It is here that we get an explanation of how the forces of self-love are actually reconciled with the larger background of social order. Pope makes clear that man is not an isolated, independent, or self-sufficient being because, by his very nature, he must be connected with larger systems. Man is bound to the earth by physical need and he is bound to other men by mutual want. In describing the second bond, the social one, Pope ventures into conjectural history. Starting with a golden age when man walked in peace with the beasts and the world was as yet uncluttered and uncorrupted by the products of pride, Pope goes on to describe the rise of man as inventor of the arts, builder of the city, and, finally, creator of the state. But, eventually, the state becomes corrupt as superstition grows and replaces the observance of natural law. One excess leads to another and man falls from his previous happy state. The cause of the fall is rampant self-love. Ego has overwhelmed all. Finally, man finds his anarchic fallen state intolerable and realizes he must impose restraints on his self-love by reestablishing a social order. This is not according to Hobbes's formula, however, because man is *returning* to an original state of peace and order.

> His safety must his liberty restrain:
> All join to guard what each desires to gain.
> Forc'd into virtue thus by Self-defense,
> Ev'n Kings learn'd justice and benevolence:
> Self-love forsook the path it first pursu'd,
> And found the private in the public good.[58]

Man's downfall was caused by self-interest, but out of the excesses of self-interest man rises once again.

Pope summarizes *An Essay on Man* in the following famous lines in which the whole story, from the principle of design through the character of inner man to man's eventual arrival at a permanent state of social order is told.

> On their own Axis as the Planets run,
> Yet make at once their circle round the Sun;
> So two consistent motions act the Soul;
> And one regards Itself, and one the Whole.
> Thus God and Nature link'd the gen'ral frame,
> And bade Self-love and Social be the same.[59]

With these words Pope distilled the essence of early eighteenth-century moral philosphy. Self-love and social love *are* the same.

III

SOLUTIONS
IN THE
HERE AND NOW

6

Paxton, Hutcheson, Bolingbroke, and Jenyns
Self-Interest as Moral Gravitation

> . . . self-interest, the great principle that operates in the
> political world in the same manner that attraction does in
> the natural.
>
> Soame Jenyns

We have seen Cumberland, Shaftesbury, and Butler arguing that self-interest, properly understood, serves the public welfare. All three writers depended heavily on the principle of design in reaching this conclusion. Cumberland applied it directly to interpret man's private actions and found those actions to be in harmony with the interest of society. Shaftesbury and Butler, using the mind as the integrating element between the design in nature and the pattern in man's actions, found that individual motives were controlled in such a way that, again, private actions accorded with the public interest. Each theory rested on the belief that the pervasive pattern of order existing throughout the universe applied not only to the actions of matter but also to the actions of individuals, the latter producing an order in society equivalent to the physical order found in nature.

This transfer of properties perceived in nature over to the mind and eventually into society required considerable feats of imagination, a faith in the dimly perceived and, even, in the unseen. First there is the central proposition of design, itself based on the belief that there is order and regularity throughout nature. This is a difficult proposition to prove because many of the events of the natural world do not immediately form any discernible pattern or order as they strike the senses. If the mind is to perceive order from such impressions it must be patient. It must accumulate and catalogue these impressions, and study them over periods of time before any kind of order may emerge. Such a perceived order must be the result of drawing inferences and bridging gaps in a kaleidoscope of stimuli hitting the senses. It requires conjecture, inference, and even faith in intangibles to make such diverse particulars run into generals. Second, after the mind has succeeded in perceiving an order in nature, then it must project this sense of order into new and different categories, those of the individual and of society. As long as one believed in the great chain of being, or the complete integration of everything in creation, as many of the leading minds of our period did, then this leap from nature over to man and society was not too difficult to make. Order must also apply to man and to society because man is, individually and collectively, a part of a greater cosmic whole. Surely, the architect of creation did not intend his great design to cover everything in creation and then stop just short of man. Consequently, man must be subject to laws of order which are part of those higher laws governing all creation. But in cooler moments the perfectly candid mind must have been aware that the arguments which integrated self-interest and social interest rested on less than satisfactory foundations, on qualities of things rather than on things themselves, on things felt rather than on things actually seen. Added proof was needed.

Adam Smith once wrote, "Mankind have had, at all times, a strong propensity to realize their own abstractions."[1] This propensity rests on a universal desire to find evidence in support of one's abstractions, or to find proof in the here and now for what were, originally, products of the imagination. Because there was widespread interest in the problem of self-interest and social interest during our period it will not be surprising to find writers searching for added proof that the two are the same. A belief in the principle of design is fine, but a real proof that the two interests coincide would be better.

The question was, where to explore? The most obvious place at the time was among the great discoveries being made in the physical sciences. Scientific proofs were accumulating that the physical universe is, indeed, orderly. What better place could one find evidence to support one's faith in design? Images reaching the eye through the new astronomical instruments indicated, clearly, the existence of a planetary order. And Newton had at last found the key to this order and, in fact, to all physical order in his three laws of motion. The existence of a universal order, which is the foundation of the principle of design, had received final and irrefutable proof. Newton had satisfied the desire for proof contained in the philosopher's passion for order. Design, in nature at least, was no longer an article of faith. It was fact. And the key to this fact was the power of gravity, which created and controlled this physical order. Might not a moral equivalent of gravity be found for man and society?

The prospects seemed good. Philosophers were gaining insights into a number of human problems by applying the principle of attraction to them. For example, feelings of benevolence could be explained by viewing them as a force, like gravity, which draws bodies closer together. Benevolent feelings drawing people together were seen as the moral counterpart among men of the mutual attraction felt by physical bodies.[2] And Newtonian principles were also used to explain the workings of a widely discussed and important function carried on in the mind, namely, the association of ideas. David Hume (1711–76), who is looked upon today as the greatest philosophic mind of his century, saw the association of ideas as a process with "a kind of *attraction*, which in the mental world will be found to have as extraordinary effects as in the natural."[3] In another place he noted that "the actions of the mind are, in this respect, the same with those of matter."[4] But being very unsure about the fundamental nature of cause and effect, he refused to speculate about the reasons for this effect. David Hartley (1705–57) carried the principle of the association of ideas and its similarity to the force of attraction among bodies to greater lengths in his *Observations on Man* (1749).

If the principle of gravitational attraction provided insights into such problems in moral philosophy as the nature of benevolence and the association of ideas, it is not surprising to see it applied to the important problem of self-interest and the social welfare. I will now examine several writers who saw parallels between the forces of self-interest and gravity in order to illustrate how self-interest, like gravity, produced order in the movements of bodies affected by it.

We begin with an obscure philosopher of utilitarianism, Peter Paxton, who appears to be the author of *Civil Polity, A Treatise Concerning the Nature of Government* (1703). In this work Paxton says his aim is to examine what he calls the "Marks of Order or Oeconomy" among people. Evidently, he is looking for special characteristics of organization common to all social life. Starting with man as an individual, he finds him subject to one important drive, the "pursuit of happiness"[5] or, as he describes it in another place, the desire for "Pleasure, Ease, or Happiness."[6] The motive behind this drive, clearly, is self-interest. Paxton them examines the social effects of this drive and becomes somewhat ambivalent about the nature of these larger effects. At one point he feels that self-interest "may be so intermixed with the Good of Others, or the Publick, as thereby not to be directly distinguished or regarded,"[7] and yet some pages later he says that the "actions or Designs of private men, seldom Extending beyond themselves or their own Families, rarely can affect many others."[8] Despite these seemingly inconsistent views, Paxton sees the drive of self-interest as a natural and positive element in the character of man. Self-interest, he insists, is "so far from being any defect or fault in his Nature, that it is Really and Truly the very Excellency and Perfection of it." The reason for this is that God has created us free agents and, as such, we have the power to decide and act in furthering our private welfares.[9] At this point, evidently wanting to place particular emphasis on the power and pervasiveness of self-interest, Paxton sees a similarity between self-interest and the force of gravity. He says that "the pursuit of happiness is as inseparable from the Nature of Man, as the Tendency towards its own Center is to unthinking Matter."[10] But he does not explore this point further. The main implication in Paxton's comment about self-interest acting like gravity is that self-interest is the central and most important control over man's private actions and, as such, must be socially constructive. Despite its short and cursory nature, Paxton's comment is worth mentioning as an early example of the application of Newton's laws to the problem of self-interest and the social welfare.

Our next writer is Francis Hutcheson (1694–1746), an important figure in advancing the idea of the moral sense found in the philosophy of Shaftesbury. Hutcheson was professor of Moral Philosophy at the University of Glasgow and a teacher of Adam Smith. He is a seminal figure in that great wave of intellectual achievement during the mid-eighteenth century usually referred to as the Scottish Enlightenment. Hutcheson's first book, *An Inquiry into the Original of our Ideas of Beauty and Virtue* (1727) breaks ground for much of the later work in ethical studies in his century.

Hutcheson devotes a considerable part of this work to refute those thinkers, such as Hobbes and Mandeville, who attempt to reduce moral judgments to motives stemming only from self-interest. He criticizes those who would "twist Self-Love into a thousand shapes," to make it serve as a single criterion for various kinds of virtuous acts. Instead, Hutcheson finds an innate and self-sufficient sense in man which approves good actions and condemns those that are bad. This moral sense exists separate from and prior to any personal consideration of one's own interest. Two people, he argues, may serve my interest equally well, but my reactions toward the one who served from his own self-interest and toward the other one who served from friendship, with no thought of gain, would differ greatly. And a gallant enemy, who obviously is not out to serve my own interest, may nevertheless receive my praise and admiration for his acts of skill and daring against me. These differences in our judgments of the actions of others are derived from a moral sense and cannot be reduced to the one criterion of self-interest. He concludes that "We must then certainly have other Perceptions of moral Actions than those of Advantage."[11]

Hutcheson likens the moral sense to the sense of beauty and harmony, or to an aesthetic sense. The sheer delight in something beautiful is an end in itself, a thing independent of all other considerations. Similarly, the approval of a good act is an immediate emotional reaction unencumbered with any other consideration. Both are the result of impulse, not reason. Considerations of personal advantage do not enter in when one wishes to share with others one's immediate enthusiasm for good art or good acts. As Hutcheson puts it, "It is an easy matter for Men to assert any thing in Words; but our own Hearts must decide the Matter."[12] He therefore places considerations of self-interest at a lower level in the heirarchy of human motives than the moral sense.

Hutcheson refers to this instinctive reaction to positive acts of others as the attitude of benevolence, and it is here that he makes first use of the gravity metaphor. "This universal Benevolence toward all Men, we may compare to that Principle of Gravitation, [which] like the Love of Benevolence, increases as the distance is diminish'd, and is strongest when Bodys come to touch each other." He then notes that if the force of gravity were the same at all distances this would stop "all Regularity of Motion, and perhaps stop it altogether."[13] The implication is that the force of benevolence must follow a law of inverse proportion with distance, or social life would be at an end. So, even the dominating motive of benevolence must be subject to control. Heart animates man but only within the background of a higher reason as imposed by a principle of attraction.

While the moral sense dominates, Hutcheson says that self-interest has an important, if lesser, function to perform in society. Man must see to his material needs, but "It is well known, that general Benevolence alone, is not a Motive strong enough to Industry." If the world's work is to be done, the lesser motive of self-interest must come into play. So Hutcheson willingly admits that "Self-love is really as necessary to the Good of the Whole, as Benevolence."[14] Self-interest serves the public welfare, if only in mundane ways. Society could not work without it. In fact, Hutcheson also sees self-interest as a motive important enough to warrant comparison with the force of gravity, as in the case of benevolence. "Self-love," he writes, "is really as necessary to the Good of the Whole . . . as that Attraction which causes the Cohesion of the Parts, is as necessary to the regular State of the Whole, as Gravitation."[15] There are big wheels and smaller wheels in the mechanics of man, but both are important to the whole, and both are subject to similar laws of nature.

Students of economic thought sometimes study the works of Hutcheson to find economic ideas which may have influenced Adam Smith, who was Hutcheson's pupil. Although similarities can be found in certain of the economic ideas of Hutcheson and Smith, the two writers separate on the important question of the economic policy of government. Hutcheson prefers a considerable role for government in stimulating industry and guiding the economy,[16] while Smith, of course, argues for strict limits on the economic functions of government. Hutcheson's mercantilistic policies might have been partly the result of his placing the function of private interest in a secondary position in his conception of social life.

A famous and controversial contemporary of Francis Hutcheson, Henry St. John, Lord Bolingbroke (1678–1752), also uses the gravity metaphor in his writings on self-interest. Bolingbroke rose rapidly at an early age to a position of high political power in the Tory party. After the downfall of the Tory government in 1714 he fled to France from fear of reprisals by the reigning Whigs. He returned to England in 1725 and spent most of the rest of his life there acting as head of the extraparliamentary opposition to Walpole and the Whig party. Bolingbroke is not looked upon today as one of the leading moral philosophers of his day. His intrigues in politics seem to have tarnished his image as a scholar. But his works do reflect some of the major concerns among writers and intellectuals of his day on certain points of philosophy.

Bolingbroke took a middle position on the nature of man. On the one hand he identified self-love as the basic motive in man, but on the other he accepted an important role for reason. He reconciled these two motives in the following way. Reason is slow and requires time to have effect, so nature has "implanted in us another principle, that of self-love, which is the original spring of human actions, under the direction of instinct first, and of reason afterward."[17] Bolingbroke summarizes this point: "We desire by instinct, we acquire by reason."[18] Self-love motivates, but reason guides this drive into useful directions. Pope was influenced by Bolingbroke on this point about self-love and reason, which is, as we have seen, a major theme in the *Essay on Man*.

"Self-love," Bolingbroke writes, "directs us necessarily to sociability. Self-love operates in all these stages. We love ourselves, we love our families, we love the particular societies to which we belong, and our benevolence extends at last to the whole human race." Self-love is transformed into social interest as it spreads out into society in ever-increasing circles from the individual. At this point Bolingbroke approaches very closely to the gravity metaphor. "Like so many different vortices, the centre of them all is self-love, and that which is the most distant from it is the weakest."[19] Again, as with gravity, we see the inverse proportion between the intensity of the force and the distance from its object.

Bolingbroke makes one other reference to an interest-gravity parallel. In discussing similarities between the worlds of matter and of men he uses analogies between "animated and inanimated" bodies. The animated bodies, which include men, "have by instinct, a sort of moral gravitation to one another, by which they adhere together in society." He likens this to the force in the material world which is "as unknown as instinct, [but which] produces a gravitation of the several part of matter to each other, and keeps them together in a kind of physical society."[20] Very clearly, man in society is subject to a force of moral attraction just as physical bodies are subject to gravitational attraction. He then goes on to describe how all bodies, both animate and inanimate, constitute one grand socio-physical-design covering all creation, and this grand design is controlled, physically and morally, by a central force of attraction.

Paxton, Hutcheson, and Bolingbroke used an analogy between the motive of self-interest and the force of gravity largely to reinforce a point already made in their philosophies, namely, that self-interest has a power and pervasiveness in the social world much like that of gravity in the physical world. But none of these writers overdid the point. They used it largely as an added comment to illustrate better the properties they felt they had already found in self-interest or, in some cases, benevolence. Our next writer, Soame Jenyns (1704–87), in contrast, takes up what had been an allusion to self-interest and gravity and reads it almost literally as a text. He includes it among several parallels he feels he has discovered between the material and moral worlds, and willingly pushes it into conclusions which earlier writers had hardly dared approach. An idea that may have been a useful stimulant to lift the thoughts and prose of earlier writers about self-interest becomes, for Jenyns, a drug transporting him into the most tenuous and remote speculations about the nature of man and society.

Soame Jenyns was born in London. He entered St. John's College, Cambridge, in 1722 and, after leaving, carried on a life of literary pursuits for a number of years. He was chosen a member of Parliament for the county of Cambridge in 1742 and served with that body until 1780. In 1775 he was appointed to the Board of Trade and Plantations. Jenyns's writings range from light poetry through serious papers on the causes of inflation. He also wrote about the unrest in the American colonies and even on theological matters. He seems to have been a popular figure in society, enjoying a reputation as a conversationalist. His writing and ideas reflected currently fashionable topics making the rounds in intellectual circles during the middle eighteenth century.

Jenyns is remembered mainly for one work, *A Free Inquiry into the Nature and Origin of Evil* (1757). This is not because of the quality of the work itself but because of Samuel Johnson's scathing review of it.[21] Jenyns is remembered more as a target of famous invective than as a source of great thought. Jenyns's primary purpose in the *Free Inquiry* is to explain why evil exists, and under this question he eventually takes up the problem of self-interest. In order to understand Jenyns's attitude toward self-interst we must first examine his emphasis on the great chain of being because it is from this concept that he gets his theory of evil, and from this, in turn, his interpretation of self-interest. As we have seen, the great chain of being is an idea connected with the principle of design. Jenyns says, "No system can possibly be formed, even in the imagination, without a subordination of parts. . . . This is in the very essence of all created things."[22] In the cosmic hierarchy of all things there is a place for animals, each species having "various degrees of understanding, strength, beauty, and perfection."[23] No one member of the chain can possess all qualities to perfection because this would end the subordination of the parts of the chain. The system could then no longer exist. Consequently, each member must lack attributes enjoyed by a higher member of the chain. A dog, for example, does not have the intelligence of a man, but a man, in turn,

71

does not have the eternal life of an angel. The "beauty and happiness of the whole depend altogether on the just inferiority of its parts, that is, on the comparative imperfections of the several beings of which it is composed."[24] Jenyns summarizes his concept of the great chain by describing it as "a large and well-regulated family" each member of which exists in proper subordination to his betters, and each enjoying certain privileges and carrying out certain responsibilities in his station.

To Jenyns, evil is really the lack of higher attributes. It is the absence of a higher degree of perfection. Evil is not a positive presence but something arising from the absence of higher qualities enjoyed by members at higher levels in the chain. It is, Jenyns says, "the absence of some comparative good."[25] And, as already noted, this existence of imperfection is absolutely necessary in order to preserve and maintain all created beings. No imperfection, no creation.

Pain, a natural evil, is, for example, necessary to make us aware of the need to take measures to preserve our bodies.[26] Suffering is, as he puts it, the "necessary taxes" to support the great design. And, a state of ignorance in the lower classes is also a necessary evil because it is "the only opiate" capable of making the laboring classes insensible enough to endure the drudgery of their lives.[27] Too much education is a bad thing. It upsets creation.

Keeping the above necessities in mind, Jenyns now comes to self-interest. Men, being imperfect creatures, must be something less than morally perfect, "neither wise nor honest enough to pursue their common or mutual interests without compulsion."[28] They "will never submit to each other merely for the sake of public utility."[29] To offset this lack of feeling for the public welfare, nature has implanted in men a special and powerful motive. It is self-interest. Men, Jenyns says, "can be governed by nothing but the fear of punishment or the hopes of reward; that is, by self-interest." Then Jenyns, stimulated by his faith in cosmic determinism, raises self-interest to a very high level of importance as he compares it to the dominating physical force in creation, gravity. We now see the interest-gravity metaphor again. Self-interest, he maintains, is "the great principle that operates in the political world in the same manner that attraction does in the natural, preserving order and restraining every thing to its proper course by the continual endeavors of every individual to draw all power and property to himself."[30] Jenyns does not explain just how men are actually kept and to their "proper course" as they drive through the social world powered by the thrust of self-interest. Faith in an order on high is sufficient enough to justify Jenyns's belief in an order below. Intoxicated by thoughts of the eminent order of creation, he does not feel the necessity of going into detail. Because the thrust of self-interest is like the attractive force of gravity, an organized social movement of men must result.

Jenyns is candid enough to admit that self-interest can, at times, get out of control and become destructive. Robbery, murder, luxurious living may result from the drive of self-interest and are destructive of men and sometimes of society. But Jenyns, always prone to see the good side, notes that "robbery may disperse useless hoards to the benefit of the public . . . and murder free the world from tyrants and oppressors. Luxury maintains its thousands, and vanity its ten thousands." Thus in this best of all possible worlds, "the worst vices, and the worst of men, are often compelled by providence to serve the most beneficial purposes . . . and thus private vices become public benefits." But then Jenyns hedges, adding, "by the force only of accidental circumstances."[31] He is willing to recognize that these acts, even though resulting in good effects, are still bad acts, and that, therefore, certain acts of self-interest can be intrinsically bad. His belief that good can come out of evil cannot quite carry him the whole distance to believe that, under all circumstances, evil *is* good. Yet self-interest is always justified because it is a necessary and important part of the plan of creation. In any event, in the hands of Jenyns we see the earthly paradoxes of Montesquieu and Mandeville about the unseemly and baser motives of man serving the public welfare projected onto the screen of creation itself. What had been ideas thought by many to be worthy only of "coffee-house philosophers" now are elevated by Jenyns to the loftiest of speculations. Jenyns pursues acts of self-interest to their farthest limits and, even though they are sometimes found unworthy in themselves, his enthusiasm still sees them serving the public welfare and, even more important, the ends of creation itself.

In a second but much shorter work entitled "On the Analogy Between Things Material and Intellectual," Jenyns once again takes up the interest-gravity metaphor. With his overriding faith in design he discusses similarities between operations of the moral and material worlds. He says, "that there are in the elements of the material world, and in the passions and actions of mankind, powers and propensities of a similar nature, which operate in a similar manner, throughout every part of the material, moral, and political system."[32] He gives examples of this general thesis. In the material world he describes how "we see all disorders cured by their own excesses." He describes how the fiercest storms exhaust themselves, eventually subsiding, and how intense sunshine, parching the earth, creates clouds later bringing rain. "Just so in the moral world," he continues confidently, "all our passions and vices, by their excesses, defeat themselves." Excessive rage immobilizes the enraged person to prevent mischief being done, and profligate living, by causing discomfort and disease, curbs the appetites causing it.[33]

Jenyns finds that his great analogy is "still more conspicuous" between the material and political worlds.[34] In the material world, "every particle of matter . . . is actuated by that wonderful principle of attraction, which restrains, impels, and directs its progress to the destined end." And in the political world, "every individual . . . is actuated by self-interest, a principle exactly similar." Self-interest, "by a constant endeavor to draw all things to itself, restrains, impels, and directs his [man's] passions, designs and actions to the important ends of government and society."[35] He then goes on to describe how the powers of both gravity and self-interest vary proportionately with mass and inversely with distance. Individuals alone exert only a small force of self-interest but, as they group themselves into societies and eventually into empires, the force becomes greater and greater. And actions of self-interest are felt more strongly face-to-face than across distance.[36]

As in the *Free Inquiry* Jenyns is willing to admit that self-interest may at times have its questionable side. In the material world the force of gravity "tumbles us from the precipice" and "pulls down the tottering fabric on our heads." Similarly, self-interest "seduces the profligate, by the prospect of pleasure; tempts the villain by hopes of gain." But, nevertheless, just as gravity "binds together the terrestrial globe, guides the revolving planets in their courses," so self-interest "is the source of all our connections . . . that binds us together in families, in cities, and in nations, and directs our united labours to the public benefit." Without the influence of self-interest, "arts and learning, trade and manufactures, would be at an end, and all government, like matter by infinite division, would be annihilated."[37] In conclusion, Jenyns says these "amazing instances of infinite wisdom in the oeconomy of things, presenting every where an analogy so remarkable, are well worthy of our highest admiration."[38]

Jenyns was only one of a number of writers of theodicies during his time. An overwhelming sense of the beauty of creation had intoxicated other minds too, and this passion, induced by visions of cosmic order, easily found ways to justify evil in the overpowering pattern of good. Bolingbroke, perhaps better than any other writer, evokes feelings for the incomparable greatness of creation, including its evil, in his exhortation, "Read, contemplate, adore, give thanks, and be resigned."[39] Voltaire's heated reaction to such strange mixtures of thoughts was expressed in his exclamation, "Vous criez 'Tout est bien' d'une voix lamentable!"[40] To one scholar, E. M. W. Tillyard, such confusion of thoughts was the result of trying to wrench an ephemeral idea out of its proper context. He describes how the idea of the chain of being filtered down from Plato through the Middle Ages to the eighteenth century in forms "more often hinted at or taken for granted than set forth." But not being content with such a "glorious product of the imagination," the eighteenth century coarsely tried to read it literally and "ended up by making it ridiculous and hence unacceptable in any form."[41] Jenyns's work was a good example of this. By a too literal reading of the chain of being, using its meanings to

74

justify the basest of motives in social life, Jenyns arrived at the most obtuse conclusions. His work made the interest-gravity metaphor ridiculous and, consequently, reduced the idea of moral gravitation to a state of bankruptcy.

But another group of writers will approach the problem of self-interest and the public welfare from an entirely different direction and will find a realistic and much more effective answer to it. We will study them in the next chapter.

7

Derham, Maxwell, Harris, and Priestley
Self-Interest in a Distribution
of the Arts

A more perfect society admits of a proper distribution and division of the objects of human attention.

Joseph Priestley

For centuries the church condemned man for the imperfect nature of his character. Civil authority punished him for his worldly behavior. Traditionally, man was caught between a religion emphasizing his depravity and secular theories treating him as a thing rather than as a full human being. As Basil Willey put it, man's soul was "ground between the upper and nether millstones of orthodoxy and infidelity."[1] Now, however, in an age of growing freedom and inquiry, man was beginning to see the lifting of some of these burdens from his past. In the minds of some writers, at least, his character was interpreted differently; it was starting to become that of modern man.

But, as yet, he had not become modern *economic* man. We have seen our moral philosophers working to raise the status of mankind by urging man to consult his own initiatives and desires. Most of their work, however, did not direct itself toward the details of how man makes a living or, more specifically, toward his economic motives and actions. The philosophers' interest was in the whole man, in his complete character, in his entire being as an individual and as a member of society. Economic motives and actions of man were included in this larger analysis but they received no special attention. Our moral philosophers had succeeded in elevating the importance of self-interest but they had not yet become aware of the great economic implications of self-interest.

These broad and balanced approaches toward man began to change somewhat when it was realized that the whole man cannot subsist on his wholeness alone. The higher pleasures of life and the cultivation of artistic and scientific aptitudes are all well and good. But they depend, first of all, on a proper economic life. The basic necessities of life must be supplied first, and supplied in the correct way, before man can cultivate higher things. Our philosophers had discovered a new morality based upon man's natural propensities. It was now necessary to discover an economic life worthy of this new morality. A morality based upon nature called for an economic life also based on man's natural propensities.

76

What would be the requirements for such an economy? On what principles should it be constructed? First, and most obviously, it must be productive. It must adequately supply the basic necessities for a reasonable level of living, plus a surplus to support the growth of a civilized life. Building the good life cannot be accomplished in famine and poverty. Second, such an economy must allow scope for man to exercise his natural motives, so recently discovered and made free by our philosophers. In short, the private interest of the individual must be made to agree with an adequate material welfare for all. How were these two goals to be reached? As we will see, they were to be reached through a simple economic principle, the division of labor.

Today, the division of labor as an economic principle is largely taken for granted. It is viewed as a simple and easily understood principle concerned with the organization of labor to increase productivity, lower unit costs, and, it is hoped, to raise profits. It deals largely with the physical procedures of workers in the factory or office. For certain eighteenth-century minds it was not taken so much for granted. For them, it evoked lofty thoughts and, in some cases, eager anticipation about its eventual effects on society. These minds not only saw it as a necessary means to meet the material needs of the population but, more important, as a principle of great social importance to the future of man, one which would allow nature to fit the individual into his destined function in society. Some saw the division of labor as the means by which man himself would reach his greatest fulfillment. To say the least, great expectations were riding on the principle.

Even though the daily labors of man are onerous, often assuming the meanest of forms, it was felt that specialization could raise man's efforts to a much higher level of meaning and importance. The reasoning was the following. The idea of plenitude implies that all available space in creation must be occupied, that each niche in creation must be filled with its own special form or type. What did this imply for the economic life of man? The answer was an economy filled with workers doing an infinite variety of things, or an economy built upon the division of labor. The individual follows his own talents and interest. Each is a specialist in doing what he does best. Thus, the individual fits into his special niche in the economy just as mankind itself and other forms in nature fill their respective niches in the pattern of creation. And, at the same time the material needs of society are being fulfilled by the increased output from specialization. An eighteenth-century faith in a differentiated nature called for an economy built upon differentiated labor. The result was a moral philosophy looking toward the division of labor, another case of an ideal searching for its reality.

We have arrived at an interesting and provocative situation in the history of ideas. We are witnessing a philosophic problem seeking an economic solution. But, as yet, there exists no formal science of economics to provide guidance for a solution. The philosophers are on their own. The problem is clearly philosophic because it concerns the inner nature of man, his motives, and his position in the processes of creation. Just as clearly, the answer is being sought in economic terms because it is concerned with the earthly processes by which men deal with material resources as they make a living. Philosophic minds in their continuing search for a solution to their problem of private interest and the public welfare are now beginning to move in the direction of what we would today call economics. These minds did not realize this because they were not those of economists. But their explorations were carrying them into new areas of thought which, when fully developed, would be called economics.

Who were these writers? They are seldom seen today because they stand in the shadow of Adam Smith's brilliant treatment of the division of labor. We will have to shade our mind's eye from the glare of Smith if we are to make out the work of these moral philosophers on the division of labor.

Another problem in identifying these writers is that their work can become lost among the many comments of others on the division of labor. Bernard Mandeville is well known and was a very early, if not the first, writer to use the term "divide" to describe the separating of employments in the division of labor.[2] Turgot refers to the principle as the "separation of different labors,"[3] Hume as the "partition of employments,"[4] and Ferguson as the "separation of the arts and professions."[5] Addison and Steele, Montesquieu, and others discuss the division of labor but in more general terms. The principle was a virtual commonplace before Smith raised it to such great importance. Smith may have had the final word for his century about the division of labor, but he did not have the first words, and some of the first ones were important, as we will see.

Our writers will use the division of labor to answer a problem in philosophy. They should not be confused with others approaching the principle strictly from an economic or business point of view. In order to avoid mixing these two viewpoints and, therefore, confusing them, we must identify each so they can be separated.

These two views toward the division of labor can be separated largely on the basis of the effects of the principle. The economic or business view saw specialization increasing the productivity of labor, reducing unit costs in the firm, and increasing profits for the employer. Sometimes these microeconomic effects were projected onto the larger screen of the economy where they were used to illuminate discussions about such questions as levels of national employment and national competitiveness in world markets. A good example of such a business or economic interest in the division of labor occurs in the *Spectator* when Sir Andrew Freeport, borrowing from Petty, describes how specialization greatly facilitates making the parts of a watch, consequently speeding up manufacture and increasing profits. He expounds on the advantages of the division of labor to the British businessman in all lines of production, knowing full well how important profits are to a healthy economy. He argues that a widespread promotion of the principle of specialization would stimulate exports and favor the entire nation through trade. At the same time as specialization lowered unit costs throughout the nation, prices would fall to lower levels and this would give the British businessman the opportunity to cut wages. Yet the workers' level of living would not suffer. Consequently, the division of labor benefits the individual businessman as it benefits the entire nation.[6]

The second view of the division of labor is very different. It does not look to purely economic effects but to the social effects of the principle. The economic advantages of specialization are all well and good, but what concerns our philosophers is the effect of the principle on the character of man and on the forming and perfecting of society. Again, we will see these considerations posed in terms of our traditional problem of self-interest and the public welfare. In using the division of labor as a means to solve this problem they will raise what is, essentially, a mundane principle onto a lofty level of society theory. This is not say that our philosophers were merely elevated Freeports. Surely not. But we will find, nevertheless, that an idea interesting to the mind of a Freeport will also become interesting to minds dealing with a problem on an entirely different level.

The modern businessman was becoming very active in the eighteenth century. The growth of trade indicates his vigor and well-being. But his status and social position in the opinion of educated minds was open to question. Political man, in contrast, could look back to a long and distinguished history in which his genealogy had been traced by leading minds. His historical credentials usually stood him in good stead in the opinion of others. But the lineage of economic man remained circumstantial and obscure. Defoe, Addison, and Steele had attempted to show that economic man deserved something better than the condescension of his self-appointed betters, but their labors on his behalf had little effect on the opinion of their times. Our philosophers of the division of labor will attempt to provide for economic man credentials worthy of those of any other personality type in the history of ideas.

I will discuss four writers who approached the division of labor from this philosophical point of view. They are William Derham (1657–1735), John Maxwell, whom we have already met as translator of Cumberland's *Trea-*

tise of the Laws of Nature, James Harris (1709–80), and Joseph Priestley (1733–1804).

William Derham was born at Stoulton, near Worcester. He attended Trinity College in Oxford and, after receiving his degree, spent much of the rest of his life as vicar at Upminster, Essex. He not only tended to the spiritual welfare of his parishioners but, as a physician, saw to their bodily needs as well. Derham developed a great interest in natural history and accumulated large collections of birds and insects. He contributed papers to the Royal Society on such subjects as the weather and the habits of insects and animals. He was elected fellow of that organization in 1702. Having developed a reputation about matters in natural philosophy, Derham was called from his rural parish in 1711 and 1712 to give the Boyle Lectures. Robert Boyle was the great seventeenth-century physicist and chemist who saw the study of science as a religious commitment and, in his will, left an endowment to support an annual series of lectures or sermons "to prove the truth of the Christian religion against infidels."[7] Although he did not specify methods to be used to present these proofs, the early lectures emphasized arguments drawn from science. Derham published a book in 1713 entitled *Physico-Theology*, which was drawn from his lectures. His most famous work, it went through many editions until the end of the century and was translated into French, Swedish, and German. It is a compendium of many of the popular scientific and theological beliefs of its day and also contains prevailing attitudes toward the nature of man and his place in society.

Physico-Theology is an encyclopedia of the products and processes of the world of nature. Derham ranges confidently from the heavens down into the depths of the earth, exploring the animate and the inanimate, as he catalogues the complexities of creation. Plants, insects, and animals are described in intricate detail in order to illustrate their clever construction that fits the designs of nature. Tides, winds, even the explosive force of volcanoes are described, and their place in nature explained. Derham finds nothing amiss. All is part of a great design. From the smallest to the largest, from the simplest to the most complex, he examines the products of the world to prove that such stupendous variety is a sign of underlying order. It is impossible, he argues, that all this could be a matter of chance. Clearly, it points toward a plan, to a great designer. The more scientific investigation reveals of this immense variety in nature, the better proof we have of the existence of the great designer. To Derham, science gives sight to religious faith.

If the physical world is filled with a vast multitude of forms and types, what does this imply about the character of man? Believing whole-heartedly in the principle of design, Derham has no difficulty in answering such a question. It is evident that variety in nature implies the same for man. In a section of *Physico-Theology* entitled "A Survey of Man," he investigates those inner parts of man "having a particular tendency to the management and good order of the world's affairs."[8] One of these parts of man is the "various *genii, or inclinations of men's minds* to this, and that, and the other business" of the world. These inner propensities for work are as various as the many forms composing the natural world. Derham then describes how men, following these propensities, set themselves to work at many different employments. We have now reached the division of labor. "We see," he says, "how naturally men betake themselves to this and that employment: some delight most in learning and books, some in divinity, some in physic, anatomy, and botany . . . , some in mathematics . . . ; and some have their delight chiefly in mechanics, architecture, war, navigation, commerce, agriculture; and some have their inclinations lie even in the servile offices of the world."[9] A diverse nature points to a diversity among men.

The wonderful result of all this is that the different drives of each individual are made to serve the larger needs of society. Derham enthuses as he writes, "all this is an admirably wise, as well as most necessary provision, for the easy and sure transacting of the world's affairs, to answer every end and occasion of man . . . and all, without any great trouble, fatigue, or great inconvenience to man. . . . For so far it is from being a toil . . . [it] becomes pleasant to him who is pursuing his *genius.*"[10] We should, then, not neglect our "stewardship, our craft, our calling."[11] It should be discharged with care and fidelity. We can do no less under nature's grand plan.

Derham is important not for repeating the idea of men being "called" to their various occupations, an idea which has been part of Puritan principles for years, but for his use of an economic principle to coordinate self-interest with the public welfare. Each individual has a special interest or inclination deep within his soul, planted there by the feature of differentiation in the design principle. To satisfy this drive is, obviously, in the person's self-interest because the result is pleasure. At the same time that the person is serving his own interest he is, by his labors, serving the needs of a larger number, and thus he is really serving the public welfare. Derham makes the division of labor the connecting link between self-interest and the welfare of society, and, in doing so, provides an economic answer to what was becoming, as we have seen, a classic philosophical problem.

But Derham's economics stops there. He does not go on to analyze the next and inevitable step after specialization, which is the process of exchange or trade. He does not explain just how the products and services of each worker are to be exchanged for those of others in order to serve the collective interest. He does not complete the economic explanation connecting the fulfillment of the individual with the larger welfare of society. He uses an economic principle, the division of labor, to solve the problem of private interest and the public welfare but does not trace out the market implications of the principle. Perhaps he felt that exchange would take care of itself and needed no explanation. Derham was not an economist.

Derham is, nevertheless, important to modern economics because he takes a common economic principle and makes it a key to a theory of society. He raises the division of labor to a level of discussion it had not enjoyed before. Discussion of the division of labor at this time was carried on largely by the Freeports of the world and proved interesting to minds mainly concerned with profits, productivity, and balances of trade. If consideration of the division of labor had continued as merely a business principle, interesting mainly to the Freeports, it is highly unlikely it could have attracted the attention of social theorists. Modern economics, when it arrived, was the work of minds oriented toward theories of society, not just toward profits and productivity. Derham introduced a new world view toward the division of labor. It will later prove to be important to Adam Smith.

Our next writer, John Maxwell, approaches the division of labor somewhat differently than Derham. His approach to the principle is not as person-oriented, with emphasis on the differentiated drives of people. But, as we will see, his approach continues to be that of a philosopher.

Maxwell's comments about the divsion of labor occur in the one significant criticism he directed at Cumberland's *Treatise*, a criticism published with his translation of the work. It reflects an increasing secularization of attitudes toward the problem of how private interest is coordinated with the public interest. Cumberland had treated the problem in very general and abstract terms, only rarely touching down into the realities of economic life to argue that the two interests are coordinate. This approach did not sit well with Maxwell. He says in his criticism: "I think our Author [Cumberland] is abundantly *too general* . . . and that he should . . . have shown more *particularly*, 'How the most of our *Enjoyments* are *general* or *extensive* in their Use,' and, '*That publick* and *private Happiness* are so *interwoven*, that the very Actions which promote the private Interest of any particular Person, do in all, at least in all common Cases, necessarily tend to the Advantage of the Publick: *That* our *Possessions* of all Kinds, and Lands, our Houses, our Money, are all *enjoy'd* by many.'"[12] Maxwell seems to be saying that a person's goods and money are not normally consumed in a purely exclusive or miserly way; that others, whether friends or businessmen, also benefit from one's wealth. Consequently, private happiness in one's material possessions spills over onto others, and the public happiness is served.

After establishing the extensive effects of private wealth, Maxwell uses this as a pattern to explain how the labor of the individual also spreads out into society. "Our *bodily Labour* too," he continues, "is always *general* in its Use: We can't so much as plant a Tree, or manure a Field, but thousands reap the Fruit of our Labors." At the same time, however, "we are utterly *unable, without Assistance*, to *provide* for ourselves the most *simple Necessaries*." For example, "The most ingenious Mechanick would not, perhaps, be able of his own Labour, to furnish himself out so much as a commodious Garment." The reason is that his labor, being specialized, goes to another purpose. How is the mechanic to be clothed? The answer to this problem is, obviously, trade. But Maxwell does not mention it explicitly. To emphasize his point about the mutual dependence of all in a system based on the division of labor, he asks rhetorically, "*Who*, I say, that yields but the least Attention to these things, can doubt of our *Dependence*, nay, of the *Necessity* of our Dependence, on one another?"[13] "These things . . . are, I think, worthy of the most serious Contemplation; and were they but fully laid open to our View, we would have a clearer insight into the *Beauties* of the *moral World*, and be at once fill'd with Love and Admiration of its Author." He concludes by repeating his opening point, saying, "It appears, from those *Observations*, That the public Good, is in the greater Number of Cases, most plainly connected with private Advantage."[14]

Maxwell illustrates the congruity of private interest and the public welfare with examples drawn from the most common operations of daily living and, in doing this, he relies on the division of labor. Cumberland had been unwilling to bring his arguments down into everyday life, perhaps feeling it unnecessary or, possibly, improper to depict the glorious workings of nature in such common ways. But Derham and now Maxwell are not so reticent. Each, with great enthusiasm, connects a very earthly principle with the higher needs of creation. There is the well-known myth of Prometheus bringing the gift of fire down from the gods to serve the needs of man. For Derham and Maxwell, the gift of specialization was brought down from on high to serve the moral needs of man. They are overwhelmed with the great importance of the division of labor. They eagerly seize upon specialization as the principle needed to transform the common motive of self-interest into, perhaps, the single most important drive in man. They take a most ordinary principle at work in everyday life and make it into a principle connected with the cosmic destiny of mankind. The division of labor will never be the same again to the mind of the eighteenth century.

The attitudes of Derham and Maxwell toward the division of labor are expanded upon even more by James Harris, a nephew of Shaftesbury. Harris was a serious student of the classics and followed closely the ideas of Aristotle. Hume showed respect for his work, even though he felt that

Harris had an overly strong penchant for the Greeks. Harris enjoyed position and wealth. He entered the House of Commons in 1761 and was at various times a lord of the Admiralty, a lord of the Treasury, and secretary and comptroller to the Queen.

His philosophical study of the division of labor is much longer and more detailed than those of Derham and Maxwell. His work on the principle marks the culmination of efforts to raise it to very high levels of consideration in social theory.

In 1744 Harris published his first work, which was entitled *Three Treatises*. One section of this book is called "Dialogue Concerning Happiness," and it is here that he analyzes the division of labor. The "Dialogue" records a conversation between two philosophers who are searching for the sovereign good. At the beginning of this conversation they decide that the sovereign good is equivalent to happiness. The question is then asked about the kind of life that is necessary to achieve happiness. After investigating lives of politics, wealth, pleasure, and contemplation, they decide that no one of them in itself will achieve the goal. They then come to the conclusion that a new method must be used to find the conditions necessary for happiness. They decide they must begin at the beginning; they must understand the basic character of man before they can discover just what is conducive to his happiness. This approach calls for an examination of man in his beginnings, in his natural state, where all nonessentials are stripped away. Borrowing an idea based upon the principle of plenitude, they state that each thing in creation is unique, or as they put it, "*Every particular Species is, itself to itself, the Measure of all Things in the Universe.*"[15] It follows that in order to know the basic character of man it is necessary to know man in himself. Evidently, the studying of the writings or pronouncements of others about his character will not do. It is necessary to go to the source, man as man.

After deliberation, they feel that they have discovered two necessary and inescapable features of man as he exists in a natural state. First, man has a need for basic necessities to support physical life and, second, a need for a life in society. These two needs, and how man must go about satisfying them, best define the character of man.

Our philosophers then take up the need for basic necessities. They find it natural for man to strive to improve the quantity and quality of his supplies. It follows then, as he shifts from, say, acorns to bread, that he must develop several arts, the most obvious one being the baker's. But prior to the baker's art there must be developed the arts of the farmer and the miller. "*Three* Arts then appear *necessary*, even on the *lowest* Estimation" to supply just the one item of bread. But this does not end the growth of the arts connected with the one item, bread. The farmer, miller, and baker must have tools and equipment, and these must be produced by other specialists. To emphasize the proliferation of arts around one simple product, one of the philosophers asks, "What a *Tribe* of Mechanics then, . . . are advancing upon us?" The answer is, "Smiths, Carpenters, Masons, Mill-wrights. . . . Not less than *seven* or *eight* Arts, we find, are wanting at the fewest."[16] And if man is to be supplied with all three of the basic necessities of life (food, clothing, and shelter), they estimate that no fewer than twenty arts are necessary.

But now the dialogue turns to a serious problem. An individual working alone is unequal to the *"Exercize of these twenty arts."* Consequently, "a *solitary, unsocial State can never supply tolerably the common Necessaries of Life."* More than that, if we pass from "the *Necessaries* of Life, to the *Elegancies?* To Music, Sculpture, Painting, and Poetry . . . to the large and various Tribe of *Sciences?* To Logic, Mathematics, Astronomy, Physics?"—what then? Again, the answer is that no one person acting alone can master them all.[17] What must be done? The solution is a *"Distribution*—Let one exercize *one* Art, and another a *different*—Let this Man study *such* a Science; and that Man, *another*—Thus the whole *Cycle* . . . may be carried easily into Perfection."[18]

But another problem comes up. If each person spends his time on only one product, how are his other needs to be supplied? The answer is that artist will trade with artist, "each supply where he is *deficient,* by exchanging where he abounds; so that a *Portion of everything may be dispersed throughout all."*[19] Interestingly enough, the philosophers see that, as man is taking care of his physical needs through trade, he is also moving to satisfy his other basic need, that for a life in society. Community living arises due to economic interdependence. Our philosophers confidently see "a new Face of things. The Savages, with their skins and their Caverns, disappear. In their place . . . behold a fair *Community* rising. No longer Woods, no longer Solitude, but all is *Social, Civil,* and *Cultivated."* To society "we owe, not only the *Beginning* and *Continuation,* but the Well-being, and . . . the very *Elegance* and *Rationality of our Existence."*[20]

The philosophers have now reached the end of their quest. They are in sight of the sovereign good, the happiness of man. The ultimate state which produces this happiness is, they pronounce, *"Commutation* and *Traffic."*[21] Fundamentally, man is a creature of the activities required to satisfy his physical and social needs. These activities themselves constitute his highest happiness. It is clear that the drive behind his activities is one of self-interest. As he acts to satisfy his material needs he also is satisfying his need for a life in society. Self-interest, acting through the division of labor, leads to the public welfare. In their search for the sovereign good our philosophers have discovered a prototype for modern economic man.

Hobbes also defined basic man as a creature of movement and action.

But where the self-interest of the Hobbesian man drove him into direct and often violent confrontation with others, Harris's basic man directs his attack against economic resources as he applies his specialized labor to land and materials in order to satisfy better those needs which define his very being. In contrast to the violence of Hobbesian man, this violence is aimed at economic resources as the individual strives to reduce their refractory qualities into useful products and services. Each of these men is a man of action but the targets of their attentions are fundamentally different. As a result of his self-centered concentration on products, and especially on one product, Harris's man is carried into a life in society. This is the result of the natural course of events because men are born with differing talents; the talents lead to specialization, and then trade must follow.

Harris employs the division of labor to prove that self-interest moves in parallel with the public welfare. But he supplements this modern economic proof of the congruity of the two interests with an older proof, one which sounds very much like it came from Shaftesbury. He introduces a third philosopher into the "Dialogue" in order to present this added argument. His name is Theophilus and, as an older and much more experienced mind, he is looked up to by the first two characters in the conversation.

Theophilus is bothered by the self-deprecatory head-shaking he sees when someone announces the sad but true fact of life that men are governed by narrow self-interest rather than by higher motives. Attacking such negative attitudes, he says sharply, "And what do they think should govern us else? Our Loss, our Damage, our Disinterest?—Ridiculous indeed! We should be Ideots in such case, more than rational Animals."[22] The real question, he explains, is not concerned with the existence of self-interest or its base nature, but rather with *where* our self-interest truly rests. He argues that any genuine interest of the individual has to be connected with the interests of others. "*If I seek an Interest of my own, detached from that of others; I seek an Interest which is chimerical, and can never have Existence.*"[23] He then asks, "Is a Social Interest joined with others such as Absurdity, as not to be admitted?" Answering his own question, he replies, "I pass from my own Stock, my own Neighborhood, my own Nation, to the whole *Race of Mankind*, . . . Am I not *related to them all*, by the mutual Aids of Commerce; by the general Intercourse of Arts and Letters; by that *common Nature*, of which we all participate?" If this social order were "once confounded I could not probably survive a Moment; *so absolutely do I depend on this common general Welfare.*"[24] Harris finds it unthinkable, even impossible, to consider the individual without considering the many. Self-interest and the social welfare necessarily run together. It is impossible to consider one without the other.

But Harris devotes most of his attention in the "Dialogue" to the proof, based upon the division of labor, that self and social welfare are the same. He far surpasses Derham and Maxwell in explaining the details of this kind of proof. But that is not enough. He evidently feels it necessary to give proper credit to the past. He feels it necessary to add the older, more general argument for the problem.

Our final writer seeking the secular salvation of man and society in the division of labor is Joseph Priestley, theologian and famous experimenter in electricity and chemistry. Priestley came from a dissenting family, was educated in conventional grammar schools and Daventry Academy, an institution set up to provide university-level instruction to Nonconformists. He entered the ministry and served several congregations before taking a post as tutor of languages at Warrington Academy in Lancashire. Priestley was elected Fellow of the Royal Society mainly for his writing on history. Although he was heavily involved in theological matters, he is remembered today mainly as an early discoverer of oxygen. His unorthodox religious beliefs and radical political views led to controversy with established authority. He sympathized with the French revolutionists in their attack on the antiquated institutions in France holding back the progress of man. English public opinion, reacting against the excesses of the revolutionaries and against radicalism in general, rose against dissenters and, in 1791, the mobs of Birmingham burned dissenting chapels and ransacked Priestley's house, destroying its contents, including his books and scientific apparatus. In 1794 Priestley left for America, where he remained the rest of his life.

Among Priestley's many publications is a work entitled *An Essay on the First Principles of Government* (1768). It strongly supports an ideal of human diversity. Priestley believes that neither the individual nor society can improve as long as personal beliefs and actions remain uniform. To Priestley, the individual was placed on earth to improve himself, and he can do this only by venturing to be different from other men. Animals, in contrast, have a fixed and unchanging character and they could never be more than what they had always been. It was the ability to be different from each other that placed man above brute creatures and in his proper station in creation. Man enjoyed the advantage of intellect, and this superiority over animals must be exercised. Intellect allowed him to study the past, understand the present, and plan for the future. Man was capable of changing himself and his surroundings and he could, therefore, make progress toward a better state. This progress depended on a willingness to be different and this could come only out of human diversity. It could never result from uniformity.

Pursuing this point, Priestley writes that the "great instrument in the hand of divine providence, of this progress of the species toward perfection is *society*."[25] Society is the prerequisite for progress because it makes human diversity possible. When man lives in a presocial state, alone with nature, "the powers of any individual are dissipated by an attention to a multiplicity of objects." Nature forces a uniformity of activity on everyone because the struggle for a living is the same for all. As Priestley put it, "The employments of all are similar. From generation to generation every man does the same that every other does, or has done." Consequently, "general improvements are exceedingly slow, and uncertain." With the establishment of society, however, "when men are connected with and subservient to one another," there can be a "proper distribution and division of the objects of human attention," or as he put it, "one man confines himself to one single object, another may give his undivided attention to another object."[26] The powers of men are no longer dissipated and weakened as before, when they were spread over many operations. Thus "the powers of all have their full effect; and hence arise improvements in all the conveniences of life, and in every branch of knowledge." After the establishment of a system of specialization, each individual will be able to master the state of an art in a relatively short time and, therefore, will be able to spend most of the years of his life producing efficiently. And a concentration of his attention on one art will lead to his making improvements in it. If the improvements in "one art or science should grow too large for easy comprehension, in a moderate space of time," Priestley continues, "a commodious subdivision will be made. Thus all knowledge will be subdivided and extended; and *knowledge*, as Lord *Bacon* observes, being *power*, the human powers will, in fact, be enlarged."[27] Man will increasingly gain power over nature and learn to make its laws work for his own benefit.

Priestley then describes how men will make their lives ever more comfortable and civilized. Their life spans will grow longer and, what is of ultimate importance to Priestley, man's happiness will increase greatly. Carried away by his great expectations about the future, he enthuses, "Thus, whatever was the beginning of this world, the end will be glorious and paradisaical, beyond what our imagination can now conceive."[28] This greater happiness rests upon the pursuit of diversity, as the individual attempts to perfect himself. And the key is the division of labor. Without this wonderful principle, man would not have a future worthy of his being. Consequently, as the individual works to improve his material condition through specialization, society comes into being and carries man toward perfection. Self-interest, most assuredly, promotes the public welfare.

One of the most striking features of the thought of our philosophers of specialization is their unbridled optimism. This is true for the establishment figure of William Derham who saw specialization as the means by which the individual could reach his destined station in the great chain of being; for the classicist, James Harris, who saw civilization itself depending upon the division of labor; and for the scientist-theologian, Joseph Priestley, who believed that the worldly perfection of man and society rested on the same principle. Perhaps the reason for this optimism was that their various theories of man and society were based firmly in the here and now on a principle operating before everyone's eyes. The unargued presence of the division of labor throughout society must have inspired confidence that their theories were valid and that man would actually attain the high goal they held up for him. They had no need to obtain inspirations from other bodies of knowledge remote from man and society, such as physics or astronomy, to justify their confidence in the future of man. It was not necessary to strain the imagination, reaching for parallels between the forces of gravity and self-interest, as Paxton, Hutcheson, Bolingbroke, and Jenyns had done, in order to justify the common ways of man. Moral gravitation was a nebulous principle compared to the division of labor, even though physical gravitation was a universal presence. In order to see a glorious future for man, one had only to look with one's own eyes at a procedure commonly employed almost everywhere man was making his living.

The theories of these philosophers of specialization might be summarized under the belief that man's future happiness depended on getting his economic life right. If this could be accomplished through the division of labor, and there seemed to be no reason that it could not be accomplished, then everything would fall into place. The future of man would, indeed, be bright. Some two centuries later John Maynard Keynes, in a speech before the Royal Economic Society, said that economists are the trustees not of civilization but of the "possibility" of civilization.[29] Our philosophers were not economists, especially not the likes of twentieth-century economists, but nevertheless they, like Keynes, saw the "possibility" of civilization resting upon a correct organization of economic life.

IV

THE ECONOMIC SOLUTION

8

Adam Smith
The Moral Philosopher as Realist

> He aims everywhere at dealing with facts rather than . . .
> primary principles.
>
> Leslie Stephen on Adam Smith

We now come to Adam Smith, the great mind who presented to the Western world a bold and convincing solution to the problem of private interest and the public welfare. I call it bold and convincing because Smith's method of answering the problem provided the foundation for a new discipline in the world of ideas, that of modern economics, and this discipline has grown steadily in acceptance and influence since his time. Although economics has been modified and refined over time, Smith's hand in its fundamental design is still evident today. Smithian economics has survived with vigor into the twentieth century, and interest in Smith is currently higher than ever before.[1] I speak of Smith's use of economics to provide a definitive solution to the classic philosophical problem of private interest and the public welfare which faced the eighteenth century. How he accomplished this task of transferring what had been a major problem in moral philosophy over into terms of economics is the subject of these next two chapters.

Adam Smith was born in Kirkcaldy, Scotland, in 1723. His father, who died just weeks before his birth, was a solicitor who held administrative positions in government, the last one being comptroller of customs in Kirkcaldy. Young Smith proved to be a good student in the local grammar school, where he received, as part of his basic education, a grounding in the classics. In 1737 he entered Glasgow University, then rising rapidly in international reputation, and studied under a number of distinguished professors, the most influential one probably being Francis Hutcheson. The faculty at Glasgow thought very highly of Smith and awarded him a scholarship, the Snell Exhibition, tenable for eleven years, which was to prepare young men for service in the Church of Scotland. He took up this scholarship at Oxford University in 1740 but soon found the social atmosphere there uncongenial and the educational methods deficient. *The Wealth of Nations*, his major work, contains a cutting commentary about these methods, and they are the equal of similar criticisms by Edward Gibbon on the same subject. Smith seems to have spent much of his time on his own, reading widely and deeply in the Latin and Greek classics in the library of Balliol College. After deciding that he was not suited for a career in the church, Smith relinquished his scholarship and returned to Scotland in 1746.

In 1748, Lord Kames, a leading member of the Edinburgh bar with interests in furthering culture and education, asked Smith to give a series of public lectures on English literature. The lectures were a great success and gained considerable attention. They created a scholarly reputation for Smith and he was invited to join the faculty of Glasgow University in 1751. He occupied the chair in moral philosophy there for many years and in the intervals between his teaching and other duties he found time to write his first book, *The Theory of Moral Sentiments*, which came out in 1759. This work gained for Smith outstanding prominence among men of taste and literature of his time. If now eclipsed by the much greater reputation of *The Wealth of Nations*, this book, nevertheless, continues to stand on its own merits as an outstanding contribution to social theory in the eighteenth century. One of the many admirers of the work was Charles Townshend, whose stepson was the Duke of Buccleuch. In 1763, Townshend wrote to Smith offering him the post of tutor to his stepson for a period of three years with plans for travel abroad, including a handsome salary followed by a large pension for life. Smith accepted the offer, resigned from the university and with his young pupil traveled to France the following year. Here Smith met and socialized with some of the leading writers and intellectuals of the day, including members of the new school of French economists who called themselves Physiocrats. During times of leisure in his residence in France, Smith began writing a book which, eventually, developed into *The Wealth of Nations*. After spending almost three years abroad, Smith and his pupil returned to London, after which Smith retired to Kirkcaldy where he settled in for a long stay to complete writing his book.

After long years on the work, interspersed with bouts of poor health, he finally, in 1773, took the manuscript to London to oversee publication. Interruptions delayed the appearance of the work but finally the book came out in early 1776. It was very well received and the first edition sold out in six months. Smith returned home and was offered the position of commissioner of customs for Scotland in 1778. He spent the last period of his life in Edinburgh tending the duties of his office and enjoying the company of friends and intellectual companions. He died in 1790.

In taking up the problem of self-interest, Smith, as we have seen, had a long and various tradition to call upon. He could have followed any one of a number of traditional treatments of the problem. But one difficulty faced Smith in following these past treatments, and this was the abstract methods used to interpret self-interest and the public welfare. His mind turned more toward the real and the empirical and, for him, the older treatments of self-interest would not do. Cumberland, for example, had appealed directly to the transcendent laws of nature to prove that man did not normally push his actions of self-interest to the point of violence and war, as Hobbes had claimed. Cumberland's ideas would settle gently into the receptive mind of Shaftesbury, who saw the wonderful balance of nature blending into the soul of man. Such visions would cause him to argue that the balance inherent among man's passions would keep self-interest under control. Jenyns and others, impressed by the newly discovered laws of physics, would use the idea of moral gravitation to explain the beneficial effects of self-interest in society and, at the same time, to cover the darker face of self-interest with an unlimited faith in the overwhelming goodness of the Governor of the Universe. Harris and Priestley, taking a somewhat more earthbound view, would work back into conjectural history and use the visible principle of the division of labor to answer the problem of how to socialize the drive of self-interest. To an age that preferred more visible and practical solutions in social theory, the division of labor was preferable to moral gravitation which, in turn, was preferable to the idea of a balance among the passions. But the economic solution using the division of labor still dragged along with it wishful thinking connected with a Socratic dialogue and enthusiasms about the perfectibility of man. Progress had been made toward an empirical solution to the problem but much remained to be done.

Smith, while he disagrees with the methods used by the earlier philosophers, does not separate himself from them completely. I shall argue that Smith's work on self-interest is a logical extension of the work of these earlier writers on the same subject, that Smith did not abandon his philosophical past as he was using economics to gain insights into the present. True, he will condemn abstract methods of dealing with the problem of self-interest, but his work in economics can, nevertheless, be seen as a culmination of the earlier work in philosophy. Smith is a product of his time in wanting to derive from factual observation a proof for the identity of self-interest and social interest but he is also a product of past thinkers who first brought the problem of self-interest into the foreground of learned discussion. Smith's method of attacking the problem will be new, but the problem was already well established in his century.

Why was Smith dissatisfied with the abstract methods used previously to deal with the problem of self-interest and the public welfare? Why did he, for example, accuse Shaftesbury of leading his readers into a "dungeon of metaphorical obscurity" in arguing about the socially beneficial nature of self-interest? We might answer by saying that Smith was moving with his time, that he was following the growing influence of the physical sciences in rejecting abstract methods for studying nature, or that he was attracted toward ideas based on facts and experience.[2] Or we might note that, as the church was losing its grip over social policy[3] and a secular-mind public leadership was coming into power, Smith, perhaps, was reflecting this increasing influence of the lay mind in shaping social practice and theory. We also know that in this period "Prose became less poetic and poetry more prosaic,"[4] and, if modes of expression shape methods of thought, Smith may have been affected by that.

Any or all of these things may have induced Smith to prefer the empirical, but the best way to answer our question is to consult Smith himself. We want to examine that part of his work which contains his criticisms of abstract methods of thought. We want to see Adam Smith as a critic of ideas. This approach should shed some light on why he found abstract methods at fault and also help to explain why he preferred empirical methods. We will start with Smith's theory of inquiry because out of this will come his criticisms of abstract methods of thought.

According to Smith the human mind "takes pleasure in observing resemblances that are discoverable betwixt different objects."[5] The mind tries to arrange its perceptions into "proper classes and assortments." This penchant for categorizing the things that come before it is, according to Smith, an attempt by the mind to come to terms with the unexpected. When "an object of any kind . . . has been for sometime expected and forseen . . . [it] glides gradually and easily into the heart, without violence, pain, or difficulty." But unexpected appearances cause discomfort or pain and, in extreme cases, may "disjoint the whole frame of the imagination."[6] This constant striving to put things into familiar categories is an attempt to explain and, therefore, understand. It is an attempt to reduce the number of surprises and, therefore, the amount of pain.

This propensity of the mind to classify, Smith continues, applies not only to single objects coming before the mind but also to connected objects, or ones coming in a train. Normally, when two or more objects have been seen to follow one another in the past, "they come to be connected together in the fancy," and "thought glides easily along them. . . . They fall in with the natural career of the imagination."[7] But when a break appears in an expected train of events the mind becomes upset, just as when an unexpected single object appears. Such anomalies in perceptions produce pain, and the resulting agitation will spur the individual to try to resolve them. This is when the process of inquiry begins.

Smith likens this process of inquiry to an attempt to bridge a gap. The mind, he says, "feels something like a gap or interval. . . . [It] naturally hesitates, and, as it were, pauses upon the brink of this interval."[8] It then searches for some explanation to carry the imagination across the interval so that it will be able to unite disparate appearances before it. Smith describes this attempt to bridge the interval as the "supposition of a chain of intermediate, though invisible, events, which succeed each other in a train similar to that in which the imagination has been accustomed to move."[9] He then gives an example of this procedure by describing Descartes's explanation for the movement of a piece of iron toward a lodestone. This movement may be explained, according to Descartes, by assuming "certain invisible effluvia to circulate round one of them, and by their repeated impulses to impel the other."[10] Smith feels that such an explanation is "in some measure according to the ordinary course of things. Motion after impulse is an order of succession with which of all things we are most familiar."[11] Smith adds, however, that the explanation is only tentative, not proved, and he calls it a "hypothesis." But it is useful because it at least moves the mind toward some tentative understanding of the anomaly, and this reduces discomfort or pain.

One point is worthy of emphasis here. Smith sees inquiry as a process of moving from the known toward the unknown. It is the use of concepts drawn from existing knowledge to construct bridges of explanation across the gaps in the perceptions of the mind. Smith requires a solid base in the known before venturing out into explanations of the unknown. This cautious procedure is necessary, evidently, to avoid spinning facile explanations having little connection with reality. The unexplained gaps facing the mind are to be resolved only by using the existing and the proven. We have before us a mind ill at ease with unsupported leaps, the mind of an empiricist.

The validity of a hypothesis, Smith says, is measured by its effectiveness in rendering "the theatre of nature a more coherent, and therefore a more magnificent spectacle."[12] It is clear that Smith subscribes to the familiar principle of design we have seen so much of and, even more, that the design in nature, for him, is essentially simple because it can be made understandable to mankind. He underlines this latter point when he adds that the success of hypotheses depends upon their ability in "gaining reputation and renown to their authors" or a "general credit on the world."[13] In short, they must be such that they can be made familiar to mankind. This "familiarity" test for the validity of hypotheses could be challenged and is, perhaps, the weakest point in Smith's theory of inquiry. But our purpose here is to try to reveal his reasons for preferring the empirical method, not to evaluate his theory of inquiry. In summary, Smith's theory of inquiry emphasizes the importance of staying with things with which mankind is most familiar and can clearly comprehend. The emphasis is on facts and experience and away from remote speculations about the nature of things.

One of the favored devices used by eighteenth-century thinkers in their process of inquiry was analogy, and certain types of analogical reasoning conform to what Smith has been describing in his theory of inquiry. They involve the projection of an idea derived from existing knowledge over onto an unresolved problem existing in the perceptions of man. The hope is to find a parallel between what is already known and what is not clear. If the parallel seems appropriate, we may gain a better understanding about the unknown. Analogy is used to support the thoughts of the inquirer as he attempts to bridge the gap between old knowledge and what he hopes will turn out to be new. So it is not unexpected to see Smith use such a device in his own inquiries, examples of which we will see later. But, at this time, we want to examine Smith's attacks on the misuse of analogy. From his criticisms we will gain a more detailed understanding and appreciation of why he preferred empiricism over abstract methods of inquiry.

It is clear that Smith is not impressed with the results often obtained from the use of analogy, and he goes into a number of examples of these poor results. He notes the "chemical philosophy," whose practitioners reached from their regular subject matter over into problems remote from their primary concerns. The chemists failed to smooth the path for the imagination of ordinary people because of the overstretched and esoteric nature of their speculations.[14] They failed the "familiarity" test in his theory of inquiry. He relates how, supposedly, the early Pythagoreans, because they were students of mathematics, tried to explain all things by the properties of numbers, and how Aristoxenus, the musician, analysed the soul in terms of harmony. Again, these were very questionable procedures to Smith. He mentions a "learned physician [who] lately gave a system of moral philosophy upon the principles of his own art" and minds who have found "parallels of painting and poetry, of poetry and music, of music and architecture, of beauty and virtue, of all the fine arts"—again, all very questionable parallels. Smith sums up such extended mental excursions as "lucubrations of those who were acquainted with one art, but ignorant of the other," who attempted to explain "to themselves the phaenomena in that which was strange to them, by those in that which was familiar."[15] Smith finds such uses of analogy to be of little or no value as a means to create new knowledge. He would allow such "lucubrations" to pass if they are merely to give "occasion to a few ingenious similitudes." But if analogy becomes "the great hinge upon which everything turned"[16] then, clearly, this is a more serious matter. Literary latitude is one thing; attempts to advance knowledge are a more serious matter.

Smith's critical attitude toward the misuse of analogy is illustrated in greater detail when he discusses the work of Kepler, the great mathematician and astronomer who discovered the laws of planetary motions, and of Quesnay, the leader of the first school of economists, the Physiocrats. He recognizes both as first-rate minds but, for Smith, neither comes off very well in certain uses of analogy. Smith mentions Kepler's passion for analogy and takes him to task for his overuse of this method of inquiry. He describe how Kepler appealed to "arithmetic and music, plane and solid geometry . . . by turns to illustrate the doctrine of the Sphere."[17] His "passion for discovering proportions and resemblances betwixt the different parts of nature, which, though common to all philosophers, seems, in him, to have been excessive."[18] Smith gives him the highest praise, however, for his valid discoveries about planetary motion and says these were aided by Kepler's proper use of analogical reasoning as applied to movements between various categories of bodies in the heavens. When Kepler confined his analogies to the heavens he could get impressive results.[19] But when he attempted to stretch them over the too great distance separating man's arts and the movements of planets, the results proved quite fanciful. With Quesnay, who was by training a physician, the problem is quite different, at least by its location. Smith mentions how Quesnay borrowed ideas from his knowledge of the human body and applied them to illustrate policies for the body politic. He believed, Smith relates, that the "human body could be preserved only by a certain precise regimen of diet and exercize" and that any deviation from this precise regimen would result in varying degrees of disease or disorder. Projecting these ideas about the requirements for the health of the human body onto the political body, Quesnay prescribed policies of like precision, this time the "exact regimen of perfect liberty and perfect justice."[20] Smith feels that Quesnay went wrong in his analogy because it did not fit facts pertaining to politics. He says political policies that are "partial and oppressive" can often be offset by strong efforts by the individual to better himself; as a result, the political body can enjoy considerable health in spite of such policies.[21] Conditions for personal health and requirements for political health are two very different things, and similar standards do not apply to both.

From Smith's warnings about the misuse of analogy, of putting fancies and fictions in place of facts and realities, we now move to another point in his criticism of ideas; again, it has to do with the borrowing of properties from an existing body of knowledge and projecting them into areas of thought where they do not belong. This time Smith is concerned with the misuse of language or, to be more exact, the misuse of certain ideas derived from language. In this case the inquirer does not borrow concepts from nature or from the arts to carry his imagination across gaps in his perceptions but, rather, borrows what he needs from the properties of language.

Smith first takes up the problem of language in a discussion concerning Plato and other classical philosophers. He takes these philosophers to task for their doctrine of "universals or species," for their attempt to classify everything coming before man into broad categories. He goes on to explain that they felt the need for such categories because they desired to penetrate to the "specific Essence" of all things. This was important because the essence of a thing controls its effects on all other things, and one of the purposes of philosophy is to explain these effects.[22] According to Smith, attempts to force the many and various elements of nature into broad categories induce a fever of abstraction into the mind and, as common sense is left far behind, tend to make the mind lose contact with what is real. He condemns universals as a "doctrine, which, like many of the other doctrines of abstract Philosophy, is more coherent in the expression than in the idea. . . . The concept of universals," he says, "seems to have arisen, more from the nature of language, than from the nature of things."[23] Evidently, he feels that language contains a property of expansion which can be used to construct categories so broad they have no counterpart in reality. The elasticity of language is stretched beyond any useful meaning, as words are made to stand for things that do not really exist.

Smith does not limit his attack on universals only to their use by the ancients. He finds the same problem occurring in his age, as he accuses Locke and Malebranche of falling into the same error. This occurred, he says, when they attempted to explain how the mind grasps general ideas. Smith is especially disappointed with Locke because he is "that very philosopher who first exposed the ill-grounded foundation of . . . Universals." And he is also unhappy with the "ingenious and sublime" Malebranche, whose explanation of universals is, to Smith, "so strange a fancy."[24] Smith sums up his low estimation of universals by describing them as a notion which "passes easily enough, through the indolent imagination, accustomed to substitute words in the room of ideas" but which, upon closer examination, is "discovered to be altogether incomprehensible."[25]

Smith also sees a second abuse stemming from language. This time it is not a matter of exploiting the power of words to expand ideas beyond their true bounds but just the opposite, the power of words to compress ideas into too small a size. In this case language is used to reduce things down to an overly great precision and, again, reality is left behind in the process. Smith takes up this point as he turns his attention to another group of ancient philosophers, the Stoics. He accuses certain later Stoic philosophers of degrading original Stoic doctrines. This occurred, he says, when the later Stoics attempted to explain two paradoxes. The first paradox is that seemingly unequal actions are actually equal. To explain this, the later Stoics strove to see all things from the viewpoint of the Superintendent of the universe. From such a viewpoint, Smith relates, "all the different events . . . what to us appear the smallest and the greatest, the bursting of a bubble, as Mr. Pope says, and that of a world, for example, were perfectly equal." Consequently, to the later Stoics, "what we would call the great action, required no more exertion than the little one."[26] The second paradox led one to believe that happiness can never be mixed with unhappiness, that they are mutually exclusive. Again, taking the highest of world views, the later Stoics argued that "all those who had arrived at this state of perfection were equally happy," so, consequently, happiness could never include any degree of unhappiness. Accordingly, all those falling short of happiness "were equally miserable."[27] Equality in perfection points to equality in imperfection.

Smith rejects the arguments used to explain these two paradoxes in no uncertain terms: "If the first of these two paradoxes should appear sufficiently violent, the second is evidently too absurd to deserve any serious consideration." He accuses the later Stoics of reducing original Stoic doctrines to a level of "mere impertinent quibbles."[28] and calls these Stoics dialectical pedants. The reason for this, according to Smith, was their attempt to reduce the original doctrines "into a scholastic or technical system of artificial definitions, divisions, and subdivisions," which, he continues, is "one of the most effectual expedients, perhaps, for extinguishing whatever degree of good sense there may be in any moral or metaphysical doctrine."[29] Such artificialities in precision turn on the power of language to narrow arguments down to so fine a point that they no longer can have any contact with the real world.

Smith's attack on the misuse of language continues as he turns a critical eye toward authors of medieval books of casuistry. He describes how the medieval church felt it necessary to codify rules of moral conduct with great exactness and how out of these efforts came books of casuistry. Smith says that these books served no useful purpose because, he argues, it is impossible to discriminate with objective precision about matters which necessarily lie deep within the emotions of the individual. No external set of rules can always be relevant in making individual moral decisions under all circumstances. The work of the casuists, he says, served "to no purpose, to direct, by precise rules, what it belongs to feeling and sentiment only to judge of."[30] The correct response for a person facing a moral decision may change with the slightest change in the situation facing him, and no specific set of rules can effectively cover all possible eventualities. "Books of casuistry, therefore, are generally as useless as they are commonly tiresome. . . . That frivolous accuracy which they attempted to introduce into subjects which do not admit of it, almost necessarily betrayed them into those dangerous errors," and at the same time they abounded "in abstruse and metaphysical distinctions."[31] Smith is again attacking those who would exploit properties of language in order to make overly fine distinctions. Such minds wrongly attempted to project features derived from words, and only words, onto the world of facts. Once again the world of words is set at odds with the actual world.

The strength of Smith's feelings about the misuse of language is shown in his admission of a personal involvement with the problem. It occurs to Smith as he is applauding Newton's discoveries. These discoveries, he says, are "the greatest and most admirable improvement that was ever made in philosophy."[32] Newton's system "now prevails over all opposition, and has advanced to the acquisition of the most universal empire that was ever established in philosophy."[33] After these accolades, Smith hesitates as he realizes that, essentially, all "philosophical systems are mere inventions of the imagination."[34] They can be nothing more than representations of reality, and the Newtonian system, even with all its validity, can never be more than such a mere representation. It cannot stand in the place of nature because nature stands far above all else and, especially, above anything the human mind is capable of constructing. Smith now admits his involvement in attempting to make language stand in the place of reality. He admits that, in his enthusiasm for Newton's system, he has "insensibly been drawn in, to make use of language expressing the connecting principles of this one [the Newtonian system], as if they were the real chains which Nature makes use of to bind together her several operations."[35] A philosophical system can never be anything more than a construction of the mind expressed on paper, yet Newton's system has so carried Smith's imagination that his mind has almost literally tried to make it a stand-in for nature itself. Here again we see Smith warning of the seductive power of words, a power which entices writers to build systems that distort or misrepresent what reality actually is.

Walter Bagehot, that influential Victorian and author of the famous work *Lombard Street* (1873), looked back at Smith from what he considered his advanced and enlightened age. Bagehot remarked that Smith's "mind was by nature rather disinclined to anxious accuracy in abstract ideas," and he seems to have felt this to be a deficiency in Smith.[36] Yet it appears, from what we have seen that Smith knew exactly what he was doing concerning abstract ideas. If he was avoiding Bagehot's "anxious accuracy," it was to shun what Smith called a "frivolous accuracy." In short, what Bagehot saw as a defect Smith valued as a positive attribute. Smith is wary of putting too fine a point on things for fear of losing contact with the often irregular terrain of reality.

If we compare Smith's criticisms about the misuses of analogy and of language we can see a common feature in these criticisms. What is criticized in each case is the transferral of an idea from its ordinary or literal context and to a place which Smith feels it does not belong. In the case of misused analogy, an idea such as harmony, something ordinarily connected with music, is used to try to explain planetary motions. In the case of misused language, the ability of words to be stretched in their meanings to extreme comprehensiveness or to be contracted to extreme exactness is used to explain properties of things that the words really do not apply to. What is transferred may be real and can actually be seen or heard, such as the harmony of music. Or what is transferred may be abstract, such as the ideas of the comprehensive or the minute, as they are derived from language. The point Smith makes is that, if the transfer does nothing to illuminate new knowledge or if it confuses existing knowledge, then it is to be avoided. It is better to confine our inquiries to areas we actually know rather than to make unwarranted excursions in areas far beyond what common sense allows. Things are what they are and not something else. The influential philosopher Gilbert Ryle used a term which seems to fit quite well the problem Smith is referring to. The term is "category mistake," and for Ryle it means the "presentation of facts belonging to one category in the idioms appropriate to another."[37] That appears to be exactly what Smith warned against.

We have seen Smith rejecting the making of broad categories as well as attempts to make all things turn on some point of fine exactness. How does he plan to avoid such pitfalls in his own work? How does he plan to avoid borrowing properties from one category and improperly projecting them onto another? We can gain insights into how Smith answered these questions by examining his discussion about final and efficient causes.

"In every part of the universe," Smith says, "we observe means adjusted with the nicest artifice to the ends which they are intended to produce."[38] He goes on to describe how the small and efficient causes operating in the organs of a plant or animal, for example, contribute to a higher or final cause for the animal—its life. And, in a further example, he says that we can easily distinguish the movements of a wheel inside a watch from the larger purpose of the watch itself, which is to tell time. But when we transfer our attention to ourselves and want to explain the reason for an action of our own, Smith says, we often point to our intellect as the cause and say the act was caused by our reason. We disregard our lesser impulses, our emotions and passions, as the cause of the act. We attribute the act to a higher cause and disregard the immediate feelings which, Smith feels, actually brought it about. The human mind tends to strive for higher reasons to explain human actions and tends to put these reasons in place of the efficient ones that really caused the actions in the first place.

Smith offers an example of this confusing of one cause for another in a discussion about the role of justice in society. He describes how man is a social animal, how he not only finds society useful but also delights in contemplating it. For social life to exist and prosper, however, there must be justice, because force and violence would break the bond between men and society would fall apart. Accordingly, those acting unjustly must be constrained or punished in order to prevent similar acts in the future. In short, it is argued that a sense for justice rests upon considerations for society, and Smith concludes, "Such is the account commonly given of our approbation of the punishment of injustice."[39] He rejects this argument and says in reply that the motive to punish does not arise from higher thoughts above the benefits and beauties of society but rather from strong and immediate feelings aroused in others by unjust acts. These feelings against injustice spring from our identifying with the injured party and reacting in our imagination as he would react against his injurer. As Smith explains it, "we demand the punishment of the wrong that has been done to him, not so much from a concern for the general interest of society, as from a concern for that very individual who has been injured."[40] The actual cause of our disapproval of unjust acts lies in our emotions, not with a rationalization connected with the welfare of society. Thus, those causes which we often connect with the intellect obscure the real or efficient causes of our actions. As Smith puts it, "When by natural principles [i.e., our emotions] we are led to advance those ends which a refined and enlightened reason would recommend to us, we are very apt to impute to that reason. . . . the sentiments and actions by which we advance those ends."[41]

It is evident from Smith's discussion about efficient and final causes that he plans to explore problems in moral philosophy largely in terms of what he considers to be their true causes, and these are their efficient causes. He wants to concentrate on the immediate and intense feelings implanted by nature in man, and not so much on the trains of considered consequences gained by consulting the intellect. He plans to avoid confusing sets of causes by concentrating mainly on only one kind. This helps to explain Smith's bent for empiricism because he finds the efficient causes of the mind, the passions and emotions, to be that part of man's mental constitution which is the most clearly observable by experience. Just as the digestive system of an animal is more easily defined than the final purpose of the animal (its life), and the movement of a wheel in a watch can be described more precisely than the reason why the watch exists (the telling of time), so man's passions and emotions, because they stand out, can be studied with greater precision than questions about the larger meaning of man. Smith is more interested in the operations of parts than in ultimate purposes, because parts have an immediacy that purposes can never have. He is intrigued with the inner workings of things, taking the view of an interested "mechanic" rather than that of an engineer, who studies with some larger purpose in mind. Smith has read enough sweeping sermons outlining the grand and glorious purposes of society and of creation. He now wants to investigate the inner workings of man and society to see how these workings conspire to produce the grand designs alluded to.

Perhaps the best way to illustrate Smith's desire for empirical methods, or the study of immediate and visible causes, is to examine his first major work, *The Theory of Moral Sentiments*. He built this work around the principle of sympathy and he considers the operations of this principle to be based upon what is more real and observable in social life than those things used by previous theories of society. This book is usually looked upon as the culminating work in the moral-sense school of philosophy. The first major figure in this school was Shaftesbury, who argued that a natural balance inherent among the passions directed human actions into a moderate course and that this balance gave men the ability to judge between right and wrong. Butler and Hutcheson followed this line of thought and made refinements in it. These early proponents of a moral sense saw men as self-contained judges of moral actions, men as fully equipped by nature with the mental attributes to arrive at moral decisions. Each man appeared to have a "moral compass," automatically pointing toward correct decisions, as if he were literally programmed in the direction of right.

Smith agreed that man has an ability to reach correct moral decisions, but he disagreed with the process described by these earlier writers on how man reached these decisions. He refused to accept their static view of man as coming into the world already fully equipped to make correct moral decisions. He could not accept man as a kind of moral automaton in arriving at moral judgments. To Smith such a conception of man neglects the everyday process by which moral decisions are actually arrived at, because it neglects the efficient causes behind these decisions. Smith explains this point when he discusses earlier systems of moral philosophy, including Shaftesbury's. In measuring the social appropriateness of a specific emotion, he says, "None of these systems either give, or even pretend to give, any precise or distinct measure by which this fitness or propriety of affection can be ascertained or judged of."[42] Smith is not willing to allow the appropriateness of an emotion to be judged by, say, Shaftesbury's "proper balance of the affections" or by Butler's "conscience," both of which he evidently feels are not directly connected with the commonplace processes of regular living and which therefore cannot be seen and examined with precision. Smith feels that moral decisions are reached by man on his own terms rather than on directions from some higher principle. So the main purpose of *The Theory of Moral Sentiments* is to explain the lower causes underlying man's moral decisions. These can be discovered only by examing the open, ordinary, and regular occurrences of life.

What is it, specifically, that enables the individual to reach proper moral decisions? According to Smith, it is the common feeling of sympathy. This is the power of the imagination, the power of placing oneself in the position of another person and, after this occurs, to be able, in turn, to see oneself from the viewpoint of the other person. He is able, as it were, to judge his own feelings by proxy or, as Smith explains it, "We endeavor to examine our own conduct as we imagine any other fair and impartial spectator would examine it."[43] "We suppose ourselves the spectators of our own behavior, and endeavour to imagine what effect it would, in this light, produce upon us."[44] Society is the mirror in which we scrutinize our own feelings and behavior.

Smith has still to explain how this transference of feelings through the principle of sympathy actually produces socially appropriate actions by individuals. To do this he first describes a human characteristic which, evidently, he feels is sufficiently obvious to require no further explanation. This is the feeling of great pleasure when we "observe in other men a fellow-feeling with all the emotions of our own breast; nor are we ever so much shocked as by the appearance of the contrary."[45] This feeling of a correspondence of sentiments is eagerly sought after, but there is always an obstacle in the way. This is the fact that man is "by nature, first and principally recommended to his own care . . . ," and, "therefore, is much more deeply interested in whatever immediately concerns himself, than in what concerns any other man."[46] As a result, one knows that feelings for self exceed in strength those that one has concerning others; likewise, others' feelings for themselves exceed their feelings for oneself. Because men by nature seem emotional islands, it would appear difficult to bring them together. The desire for a correspondence of sentiments is stronger, however, than the inherent tendency for their remaining apart. Consequently, the individual will lower his passions for self, as Smith puts it, "to that pitch, in which the spectators are capable of going along with him." A person reduces the intensity of his own passions so that they can go in "harmony and concord with the emotions of those who are about him."[47] Or, putting it more directly, Smith repeats that a person will "humble the arrogance of his self-love, and bring it down to something which other men can go along with."[48] Through the principle of sympathy, one is enabled to adjust his feelings and actions to a level that is socially acceptable. This condition is brought about by continual emotional interactions and adjustments among individuals, which take place through the medium of imagination. Smith would put what happens in these adjustments among the very ordinary happenings of everyday life and, therefore, would place them in his category of efficient causes. But these efficient causes, clustered around his principle of sympathy, serve a higher cause, which is social life.

Smith feels that his explanation of moral decisions, as based upon the principle of sympathy, is superior to other moral systems because it "is not concerning a matter of right . . . but concerning a matter of fact." He sees his system to be based upon the facts as they exist for the "weak and imperfect creature" which man actually is, not for superior beings who could arrive at similar results through the use of reason. Man, being the creature he is, cannot usually be expected to arrive at moral decisions through his intellect and, while man has a natural desire to preserve society, "the Author of nature has not entrusted it to his reason" to achieve this end.[49] Rather, nature has endowed man with instincts and appetites which play a part in everyday human interaction to provide the means by which he can arrive at a larger end, a life in society. Man learns how to control his feelings, Smith concludes, not by listening to some "abstruse syllogisms of a quibbling dialectic" but by reacting to "the sentiments of the real or supposed spectator of our conduct."[50]

Smith's sensitivity to facts is so strong that he candidly admits his system of morality does not always produce the effects expected from it. Normally, men will react to curb extreme emotions toward each other because "Humanity does not desire to be great, but to be beloved."[51] But this is not always the case. Occasionally injustice and cruelty may prevail, because the "natural course of things cannot be entirely controlled by the impotent endeavors of man,"[52] as emotions sometimes get beyond control. The impulse to oppose sometimes overcomes the desire to go along, and society is weakened as a result. Smith has no easy answers for the occasional breakdowns in the operation of sympathy, but he is realistic enough to let his readers know that he is aware of them.

The realism of Adam Smith in his moral philosophy has been noted and acclaimed by a number of writers. L. A. Selby-Bigge, for example, commented that the principle of sympathy saw the "organic unity of social feeling based on common circumstances and conditions of life" as "a notable return to a more concrete method of thought." This was no mean achievement "in an age of facile individualism," when "men started from a conception of society as built up of individuals equipped each with a complete moral faculty." He compliments Smith by calling him "one of the least metaphysical persons that ever wrote."[53] J. A. Farrer also applauded Smith for his "appeal to the facts and experience."[54]

But Thomas Huxley, the great Victorian scientist and vigorous champion of Darwin, espoused the empiricism of Smith and his principle of sympathy in a more novel way. Starting from the viewpoint of a zoologist, he described how "Man is the most consummate of all mimics in the animal world; none comes near him in the scope, variety, and exactness of vocal imitation; none is such a master of gesture; while he seems to be impelled thus to imitate for the pure pleasure of it." Then, following these thoughts over into the emotions of man, Huxley also said that "there is no such another emotional chameleon" as man. "By a purely reflex operation of the mind, we take the hue of passion of those who are about us, or, it may be, the complementary colour."[55] That seems to be exactly what Smith was talking about: man as an emotional chameleon who, by his very nature, goes along with his social surroundings. Coming from one of the least sentimental minds in recent history, this recognition of Smith's realism is, indeed, high praise.

9

Adam Smith
The Moral Philosopher as Economist

He was . . . the mouthpiece through which the philosophy of
his time succeeded in making itself audible to the world.
Leslie Stephen on Adam Smith

The publication in 1776 of Adam Smith's great work, *The Wealth of
Nations*, drew the interest and praise of some of the greatest minds of the
period. Edward Gibbon remarked in a letter to Adam Ferguson, "What
an excellent work is that which our common friend, Mr. Adam Smith, has
enriched the public!—an extensive science in a single book, and the most
profound ideas expressed in the most perspicuous language."[1] In the
following year, in a letter of congratulation to Smith on his appointment
as commissioner of customs for Scotland, Gibbon lauded Smith as a
"Philosopher who . . . had enlightened the world by the most profound
and systematic treatise on the objects of trade and revenue" which had
ever been published.[2] Samuel Johnson's comments were less effusive but
more penetrating. Boswell brought up the question of whether a man,
like Smith, with no experience in trade should write a treatise about trade.
To which Johnson answered, "Sir, a man who has never been engaged in
trade himself may undoubtedly write well upon trade, and there is nothing which requires more to be illustrated by philosophy than trade does."
Continuing, Johnson declared, "A merchant seldom thinks but of his own
particular trade. To write a good book upon it, a man must have extensive
views."[3]

   In light of such comments by Gibbon and Johnson about Smith as
philosopher, the reader of *The Wealth of Nations* would expect the work to
be rooted firmly in the philosophic interests and attitudes of its day, and
he would not be wrong. It is a work unique for its sweeping comprehensiveness and, yet, its logical organization, a work to be expected from the
systematic mind of a philosopher. It also reflects quite distinctly Smith's
empirical method of investigation, which arises from his deeper thoughts
about methods of inquiry that we examined in the last chapter. But most
important, *The Wealth of Nations* is built upon the classic philosophic
problem we have been studying, the problem of self-interest and the
public welfare. If this problem had not been a leading issue among the
intellectuals of the day, it is doubtful that *The Wealth of Nations* would have

been written, for that was its central issue. Smith was, after all, a mind moved by social and moral issues and he viewed economics as a tool to resolve such issues. The work marks a culminating effort to answer the problem of self-interest and the social welfare and, in this respect, it is a response to earlier philosophic speculation.

Smith agrees, generally, with the conclusions of our earlier philosophers that self-interest serves the social welfare. But he cannot accept the methods they used to arrive at these conclusions. He finds those methods too abstract, dealing with forms and essences rather than with the realities of life. Smith decides that a different method must be used, that it is necessary to investigate self-interest in terms of the real and the factual, in terms of efficient rather than final causes. This interest in the near rather than the remote causes of things moves Smith to seek an economic solution to the problem of self-interest because business life is filled with plainly visible activities which are near at hand.

But once Smith insists on studying man in terms of these mundane activities, he will not be able to avoid seeing certain things that are not conducive to the public welfare. If his empiricism insists on studying the facts and details of human life, he is going to encounter some facts which do not enhance the common interest. Our earlier philosophers could often ignore such uncertainties connected with self-interest because they seldom faced up fully to the complete range of facts in everyday life. If blemishes marred the face of self-interest they could, and did, apply a metaphysical "cosmetic" to make them disappear. But Smith would not allow himself the use of such abstractions. His sense of realism forces him to examine all aspects of man, and some of these aspects will not be appealing nor will they agree with the conclusions he wants to reach in his economic theory. His insistence on as complete a realism as possible is, perhaps, the best indication of how strongly he felt about the empirical method, but it will lead to problems.

Smith is one of the leading moral philosophers of the eighteenth century, and the high recognition accorded his first major work, *The Theory of Moral Sentiments*, attests to this. But how could a renowned philosopher have written a philosophic masterpiece and then, later, come out with a work on trade, *The Wealth of Nations*? The contents of the *Moral Sentiments* shows such headings as "On the Sense of Propriety," "Of Merit and Demerit," "Of the Character of Virtue," and "Of Self-Command." *The Wealth of Nations* has headings like "Of the Origin and Use of Money," "Of the Profits of Stock," and "Of Taxes." It would appear that a mind devoted to self-improvement had deserted the world of virtue and, somehow, had been enticed by the lures of mammon. The seemingly deep division between the subject matters of Smith's two great works bothered commentators for many years; only recently, after wider and deeper

reading of Smith provided greater insights into his intellectual background, have students of Smith begun to understand and appreciate the
consistency of the two works.[4]

This previously perceived disparity between the two works arose
largely from something of which we have already spoken. It arose from
the desire of later minds to interpret Smith in terms of the categories
familiar to them. In this case it was the forcing of the broad ideas of the
eighteenth century into the narrow categories of modern economics. In
the process the old ideas were separated from their philosophic sources,
shorn of their humane features, in order to make them fit the narrow
confines of modern economics. Consequently, those parts of Smith's
economics providing connections with his moral philosophy were largely
ignored and Smith became, by later interpretation, the father of the
highly deductive science of modern economics in spite of his warnings
against abstract methods. Thus it appeared that Smith's two major works
lacked consistency. But, interestingly, the supposed inconsistencies did
not appear to be a challenge to Smith's contemporaries, such as Gibbon
and Johnson. Perhaps it was because all their minds operated on essentially common categories of thought, something that does not necessarily
occur across centuries.

The title of Smith's great work in economics, *The Wealth of Nations*, is most
appropriate. It is, in fact, a book about building national wealth and
opulence. Smith opens the work by identifying the primary source of
national wealth as the labor of the individual worker and, while later he
will also discuss other resources as contributing to national wealth, he
never loses sight of labor as its ultimate origin. This is the labor of the
individual as he carries out his usual activities for his own ends. The book
is filled with penetrating comments about people as they think and act in
their daily rounds of work. It is a book on economics but it is also a work
describing human nature, because Smith never loses sight of the individual.

In the first paragraph of *The Wealth of Nations*, Smith says, "The annual
labour of every nation is the fund which originally supplies it with all the
necessaries and conveniences of life which it annually consumes."[5] The
size of this supply of "necessaries and conveniences," or of what would be
called today the national product, depends mainly on the productivity of
the nation's labor. The productivity of labor, in turn, is determined
largely by the division of labor or, as Smith puts it, "The greatest improvement in the productive powers of labour . . . seem to have been the effects
of the division of labour."[6] The message is clear. If a nation is to develop
economically it must promote the principle of specialization in its labor
force. This is the message of *The Wealth of Nations*, and it would hardly be

too much to say that its main theme is the promotion of economic policies which will advance the division of labor. Smith never loses sight of this goal.

Smith's great emphasis on the division of labor warrants further discussion. Earlier economic and business writers were well aware of the principle and recognized its potential for increasing the productivity of labor. But they did not go as far as Smith in recognizing it as the key to building national wealth. Mandeville and Turgot may have evidenced some thoughts in this direction, but they mentioned the principle largely in passing and gave it no special place of importance in their works. On the other hand, the social theorists discussed in Chapter 7 saw the principle as all-important because they recognized it as the virtual source of social life. The first group largely ignored the wider economic implications of the principle, while the second, enthusiastic about the principle philosophically, lost sight of its hard economic meanings. Consequently, by the time of Smith, a study in depth of the real national economic implications of the division of labor had hardly been attempted.

It is not my intention here to go on and say that Smith made up for the deficiencies of these two groups in their treatments of the division of labor; that by combining the viewpoints of each he gained intellectual respectability for the principle and did this by expanding its economic treatment while toning down its treatment as social theory. Such a great synthesis is not the case, because he comes to the division of labor from one point of view, namely, the empirical one. But while his approach is that of the mind of an economist, he will, before he is through, point out some broad implications for social theory stemming from the principle. On balance, his treatment of the division of labor will be more original than derivative.

One could say that the two earlier groups dealing with the division of labor studied it largely in terms of its effects in raising labor productivity on the one hand, and in increasing social cohesion on the other. Smith, too, is interested in its effects as they influence labor productivity. What is usually much less noticed in Smith's treatment of the division of labor is his detailed exploration of its deeper causes. This is important because, when Smith explores the causes of the division of labor, he traces the principle back to its sources in the nature of mankind and, consequently, connects it with his moral philosophy. He says that the division of labor "is not originally the effect of any human wisdom" but arises from a "certain propensity in human nature . . . to truck, barter, and exchange one thing for another." He then adds that this drive to trade is unique in man. "Nobody ever saw a dog make a fair and deliberate exchange of one bone for another with another dog."[7] Smith explains that trade is carried on by engaging other peoples' self-interest because each party, whether buyer or seller, tries to make his opposite number in the transaction believe "that it is for their own advantage to do for him what he requires of them." Generous feelings do not enter in because, as Smith puts it pointedly, "It is not from the benevolence of the butcher, the brewer, or the baker, that we expect our dinner, but from their regard to their own interest."[8] Consequently, the division of labor arises from a desire to serve one's self-interest but in such a way as to engage the self-interest of others. It is, at base, connected with the emotions, that part of human nature containing efficient causes, upon which Smith places so much emphasis. The connection that Smith makes between the division of labor and his moral philosophy is now becoming evident.

But it is necessary to delve more deeply into his moral philosophy to see this connection in detail, and we must examine how the drive to trade operates within his principle of sympathy. In his *Lectures on Justice, Police, Revenue and Arms*, Smith asserts that the "real foundation" of the desire to trade "is that principle to persuade which so much prevails in human nature. When any arguments are offered to persuade, it is always expected that they should have their proper effect." Because the essence of human interaction is to convince others to go along with our own feelings, we "cultivate the power of persuasion, and indeed we do so without intending it." Smith emphasizes the importance of the power of persuasion by adding, "Since a whole life is spent in the exercize of it [persuasion], a ready method of bargaining with each other must undoubtedly be attained."[9] Thus, we have a distinct connection between Smith's central moral principle of sympathy and the desire to trade. Man is at heart a persuader, an inducer, who finds trade a necessary and convenient vehicle for exercising this propensity. It should be noted, however, that the adjustment of feelings to a mutually acceptable level, as described in the *Moral Sentiments*, takes place by lowering the "pitch" of one's passions to a level others could go along with. But in the *Lectures*, as just described, it would appear that one strives to attain a mutually acceptable level of emotions as he strives to pull up their feelings to his own level. In either case the final result would be the same, a level of feelings which both parties can go along with.

Smith also describes how his principle of sympathy is directly involved with the personal motives underlying the accumulation and display of wealth. It is obvious that trade can be very much a part of this process. Again, it is the emotions and sentiments that are the prime movers of men, not the intellect. In a discussion in the *Moral Sentiments* about the origin of ambition, Smith asks, "For to what purpose is all the toil and bustle of this world? what is the end of avarice and ambition, of the pursuit of wealth, of power, and preeminence?" He answers that "it is chiefly from this regard to the sentiments of mankind, that we pursue riches and avoid poverty,"[10] and adds, "It is the vanity, not the ease, or the pleasure, which interests us." Then, returning to his key principle of sympathy, he roots vanity in the transference of feelings among men, as he explains that "vanity is always founded upon the belief of our being the object of attention and approbation. The rich man glories in his riches, because he feels . . . that mankind are disposed to go along with him in all those agreeable emotions with which the advantages of his situation so readily inspire him."[11] In other words his wealth renders him "the object of the observation and fellow-feeling of every body about him."[12] In this situation the procedures of persuasion are not carried out face to face, as in the earlier case of bargaining, but are carried out by proxy as the rich man allows his wealth to do the persuading for him. The end result is the same because the wealth induces in others feelings which are the same as the rich man's. (Smith is assuming that actual and vicarious consumptions of wealth induce similar feelings.) It is, of course, possible to accumulate wealth by grant or inheritance, but Smith implies that trade is the dominant channel for acquiring wealth. Smith thus repeats in another way the connection between his principle of sympathy and the desire to trade, which, in turn, leads to the division of labor and economic development. His moral philosophy and his philosophy of economic development are all of a piece.

Smith offers another explanation for the pursuit of riches. It is not connected with sympathy but arises from the emotional propensity in man for order and design. Smith begins his discussion of this point by noting that power and riches are, when viewed critically, merely "artificial and elegant contrivances" or "enormous and operose machines contrived to produce a few trifling conveniences to the body. . . . They are immense fabrics which it requires the labour of a life to raise, which threaten every moment to overwhelm the person that dwells in them."[13] But when riches are viewed in a more positive light, "we are charmed with the beauty of that accommodation which reigns in the palaces and economy of the great." We are taken in by the "regular and harmonious movement of the system, the machine or economy by means of which it is produced," and, therefore, feel riches to be "something grand and beautiful, and noble, of which the attainment is well worth all the toil and anxiety which we are so apt to bestow upon it." What is burdensome and inconvenient, when viewed critically, is transformed by the emotions into something great and attractive. Man's passion for design overcomes his reason. Continuing, Smith says that "it is well that nature imposes upon us in this manner," because it is "this deception which arouses and keeps in continual motion the industry of mankind."[14] Man does not work for bread alone, which keeps only his body together; he also caters to his emotions, which keep his soul together. "The same principle, the same love of system, the same regard to the beauty of order, of art and contrivance, frequently serves to recommend those institutions which tend to promote the public welfare," Smith adds.[15] These are the interdependent institutions of government, trade, and manufactures, and we "take pleasure in beholding the perfection of so beautiful and grand a system."[16]

Smith is pointing to and emphasizing the importance of the instinct for design in man's soul and, what is important for our purposes here, he sees this instinct as a major impetus behind the personal drive to wealth and behind positive public attitudes toward institutions conducive to wealth. Man's industry arises not only from the principle of persuasion as we saw earlier, but it is reinforced by the love of design. So men see wealth not only as a means of inducing others to go along with their own feelings but also as a means of satisfying their love of system. In each instance the drive to get the world's work done arises from an intimate, personal impulse within the mind of man.

The desire to trade emanates from deep within man's character. It arises from strong and immediate impulses and is common to all mankind. As the division of labor advances in society, spurred by this universal desire to trade, Smith says that "Everyman thus lives by exchanging, or becomes in some measure a merchant."[17] Man, as he reacts to an immediate impulse, sets in motion a chain of events the eventual result of which is the development of a complex structure of institutions known as commercial society. This great and final result cannot be foreseen; it is not the result of previous calculation and planning but is propelled into being by the limited and personal acts of each individual following his own interest. Smith sees modern civilization based upon and advancing with the impulsive actions of individuals, as small acts beget great consequences.

After establishing the fundamental importance of the division of labor, Smith, logically enough, devotes much of the remainder of *The Wealth of Nations* to an analysis of those economic conditions and policies which promote the division of labor. The economic environment most conducive to the division of labor is the free market. This important point is summed up by implication in one of Smith's most quoted statements: "The division of labor must always be limited . . . by the extent of the market."[18] This means that the division of labor and, therefore, production can expand only so far as there is sufficient demand for the product. More important, what Smith is also saying is that, if the benefits of the division of labor are to be realized, markets must be allowed to expand without confinement or restraint. This means markets should be free. Maximum market freedom, of course, occurs when there are no hindrances to the entry (or exit) of producers and buyers.

Smith now finds it necessary to analyze the act of trade itself in order to understand in detail what are the required conditions for market freedom. This brings his attention to the problem of product value, because exchange will not occur until buyer and seller reach a mutually acceptable value for what they are planning to trade. Smith has now arrived at a crucial point in his study of commercial society. He is about to leave the tangible, almost tactile, world of production, where material resources are to be combined physically, and to enter the completely different world of arguments and assertions about product value. It is one thing to explain how materials and labor should be arranged for production; it is quite another to take up the problem of who and what are responsible for the value of the goods produced. A finished product as it stands alone in its sheer materiality may appear a singular thing, but how its value is determined is not a singular process. The three distinct interests of labor, capital, and land are involved in giving the product its being, and their claims on the product must be resolved before it can be offered for sale. More than that, the buyer's assertions about the product's value must be considered before the act of exchange can actually take place. The two distinct and different worlds of supply and demand must be brought together.

Smith is aware of the new and complex world he is facing, a world of abstraction. Before he enters this problematic area of product value, he prepares his readers for the difficulties to come: "I must very earnestly entreat both the patience and attention of the reader: his patience in order to examine a detail which may perhaps in some places appear unnecessarily tedious; and his attention in order to understand what may . . . appear still in some degree obscure." But he warns his readers ahead of time by candidly admitting that, after he has made his best efforts to clarify the subject, "some obscurity may still appear to remain upon a subject in its own nature extremely abstracted."[19]

It appears that Smith is about to do something he did not intend to do. As we will see, he is about to enter a search for a final cause, that of product value. As we have already noted, he wanted to concentrate only on efficient causes, but his deep interest in the process of exchange leads him in search of an absolute measure for value, which is, as he admits, an extremely "abstracted" subject. He is going to try to find the "essence" of product value, and this goes against his warnings to avoid the metaphysical and stay with what is real. Just what is Smith hoping to accomplish by this admittedly risky venture into an explanation for value? We will attempt to show that his major purpose is to define as precisely as possible those market conditions pertaining to selling price and production cost that are most conducive to the expansion of trade and, therefore, to the growth of the division of labor. Smith is venturing into economic theory in service of the division of labor, and the final result will be a technical explanation to support his advocacy of the free market.

He starts off straightforwardly enough by identifying labor as "the real measure of the exchange value of all commodities."[20] Smith is consistent here because he bases the wealth of a nation on the productivity of its labor, and it follows that the value of a product should reflect the labor that went into it. He seems to be identifying labor as some kind of ultimate determinant of value. But he runs into difficulty as he soon realizes that the effects of labor can be seen in the form of products but labor itself is intangible and, consequently, difficult to measure. Even more important, labor is seldom actually used to measure value in ordinary acts of trade. Labor may well be immanent in all products but, in the realities of trade, value is usually expressed in terms of other commodities or of money, not in terms of labor.[21] Smith is caught in a dilemma between theory and practice and never fully resolves it, because he will never completely let go of a labor theory of value.

He has arrived at what, in actual practice, is exchanged for a product, namely, other products or money, and he pursues this point. The "real" price of a commodity, he says, is "the quantity of the necessaries and conveniences of life which are given for it," while the "market" price is the "quantity of money" given for it.[22] He distinguishes between value as expressed in the direct terms of other products and value as expressed in the indirect terms of money.

He now sets out to explain the important functional relationship between real and market price, and to do this he first traces out to whom market price is paid. In primitive societies it accrues entirely to labor because labor is about the only resource specifically used in production. Thus market price becomes entirely wages. But as society advances and employers enter the scene, some part of market price must be paid to cover their efforts and the cost of their capital used in production. Thus market price is divided between wages and profits. Finally, when the landlord arrives in society, he will demand his share of the market price and a third share will be paid out to him as rent. So, market price in any advanced society is divided up between these three claimants and is paid out as wages, profit, and rent.[23]

Smith then establishes "natural rates" for these three incomes, which he describes as the "ordinary or average" rates in a given area. These seem to be the customary rates for wages, profit, and rent; ones which are neither so high that their recipients enjoy higher than expected incomes, nor so low that their incomes are significantly below former levels. He adds together wages, profit, and rent at their natural rates and this sum is equal to "natural price." He then compares natural price with market (actual) price and, if they are equal, he says that "The commodity is then sold precisely for what it is worth, or for what it really costs the person who brings it to market."[24] The market price may, of course, actually fall above or below natural price, and Smith describes the market adjustments which will take place to bring the two prices together. If quantities offered for sale are too great, market price will fall below natural price, and the product will be sold at a loss. This will force some sellers out of the market, reducing quantity offered, and market price will rise toward natural price. On the other hand, if quantities offered for sale are too low, market price will rise above natural price and the product will be sold at a higher than normal profit. This will attract more sellers and the increased quantity offered will drive market price down toward natural price. Eventually, after these adjustments have had time to work out, market price will settle down near or at the level of natural price and the market will have reached equilibrium. At this point sellers will just be covering their incurred costs and, in this absence of loss or extraordinary profit, sellers will neither be forced out of nor attracted into the market.[25] In short, supply automatically adjusts to demand, and both gluts or shortages of the product are eliminated.

Smith's detailed discussion of how a market automatically adjusts its supply to meet demand is meant to illustrate in detail how markets *should* act. The important point is that, in his ideal of the automatically adjusting market, producers are free to enter or leave and to offer to sell any quantity they desire. If markets are to expand, such market freedom is, to Smith, an absolute necessity, and we already know the important connection he makes between market expansion and the division of labor. Market price must be free to gravitate toward natural price; the wealth of nations literally depends upon it. Smith has faced up to the problems of value in order to establish theoretical norms for economic growth.

But Smith offers more than a technical justification for the free market in terms of economic theory; his personal feelings in favor of this kind of market run deep into his moral philosophy. He says, with great seriousness, "The property which every man has in his own labour" is "most sacred and inviolable. The patrimony of a poor man lies in the strength and dexterity of his hands; and to hinder him from employing this strength and dexterity in what manner he thinks proper without injury to his neighbor, is a plain violation of this most sacred property."[26] Smith is attacking the practices of businessmen and the policies of government which restrain the way in which the worker may choose to employ his labor. These restraints block the way to free markets and Smith abhors them because they strike at the very foundations of his moral conception of man. His emphasis on efficient causes leads him to a conception of man as made up of passions and emotions, and he views man's labor as an expression of these inner impulses. When business or government limits how a person can peacefully use his labor, this becomes, for Smith, a most impertinent interference into the inner being of man. It is a manifest violation of the laws of nature. Thus Smith's argument for free markets is not only a technical one, showing how such markets act to allocate economic resources most efficiently in a material sense, but also a moral one showing that outside interferences in such markets are, virtually, assaults on man's soul.

Smith accomplished what he set out to do. He was determined to move the social theory of his time away from what he considered an overemphasis on final causes and toward a greater concern with efficient causes. He discovered a proof, based upon efficient causes, that self-interest serves the public welfare. As he argued in his theory of inquiry, investigations must be conducted on the home ground of what is being investigated, and the home ground for man is the passions and activities he devotes to making a living. By arguing in this way, Smith followed his own rule of inquiry. His inquiry does not depend on nebulous qualities within man's soul, such as Shaftesbury's moral sense or Butler's conscience, which work through powerful but invisible forces of design to insure that self-interest will stay within the public welfare. And, even more, Smith does not depend on literal parallels between the principle of gravitation and self-interest to express a faith that acts of self-interest are socially responsible, as Jenyns and others did. Later philosophers who used a philosophical approach to the division of labor, like Harris and Priestley, may have intrigued Smith because they were getting close to the daily realities affecting almost everyone in society, but their metaphysical style and open-ended optimism would not have set well with a mind like Smith's. Searches for final causes such as a moral sense, moral gravitation, or perfectibility by the division of labor will not do if one wants to understand truly how self-interest works constructively in society. Man is a social animal, but theories from on high to explain this fact are futile. He is a social animal because his common emotions, pushing him toward immediate and limited goals, work to make his self-interest serve the ends of society. And the whole process occurs right before our eyes.

Cumberland and Shaftesbury had pioneered in the efforts to allow man to stand on his own moral feet and face up to the theologians and political theorists who had been keeping him down. The two philosophers provided the early efforts needed to create modern man and, undoubtedly, their work was an inspiration to Smith. Their goal was laudable but Smith could not go along with their methods and those of their successors. Pronouncements about the general workings of self-interest, which were essentially products of their intellect, were not enough; more positive details and explanation were needed. Smith explored the depths of

119

self-interest and found the mechanisms at work to be more complex, yet more visible, than had been thought. In these explorations he found that simple impulses connected with the ordinary activities of everyday living are the causes underlying the great and complicated structures of the economy and society. Smith inherited the idea of modern man from the earlier philosophers, but when he had finished his own work he had transformed their modern man into modern *economic* man.

But we have not quite reached the end of the story. Smith insisted on seeing man in all the variety of life. Perhaps he saw too much.

Leslie Stephen wrote of Adam Smith: "He never takes leave of the solid ground in his most daring flights."[27] This short comment seems the most appropriate one on which to conclude because it sharply underlines the enigma that was Smith. As Stephen implies, Smith's work may have been overstretched between his need for theory and his strong desire for facts. Here was the first truly great mind in modern economic theory but a mind which could not ignore certain intractable facts which tended to deny his theory.

During his limited flight into economic theory, Smith never took his eyes from certain practices of businessmen and politicians. As he was attempting a formal definition of free markets he was also noticing the struggle by privileged groups and classes to defeat the possibility of these markets. Reacting strongly, Smith devotes long sections of *The Wealth of Nations* to attacks on those who were blocking the practical applications of his theory. (We have already seen a few of his attacks in Chapter 2.) He knew how powerful and deeply entrenched were the practices of business and government in restricting markets, and how special economic privileges were buttressed by ancient usage, so he makes his attacks on them as strong as he possibly can. He had already appealed to his readers' sense of logic in his formal argument for free markets. He now felt it necessary to descend to personalities and stereotypes in order to inflame his readers' senses against these violaters of economic freedom. But, in the end, after Smith has used all of the tools at his command, it seems doubtful that he has succeeded in his war against economic privilege. His empiricism led him up to the problem of value and, therefore, into economic theory. Now the same empiricism raises questions about the applicability of his theory in practice.

Smith's assaults on restrictive market practices begin immediately after he has established the formal norms of the free market. He describes how manufacturing and trade secrets are used to restrict product supply, causing selling price to remain abnormally high for extended periods of time, if not indefinitely.[28] This is followed by his description of similar exploitation of the public by grants of monopoly by government, where the monopolist is enabled to charge the highest price that "can be squeezed out of the buyers." Finally, in these early attacks on economic privilege, Smith takes up the exclusive powers of corporations and statutes of apprenticeship which allow groupings of businessmen to form "enlarged monopolies" and thus to control market supply on an even larger scale than in the above cases.[29]

But Smith saves his strongest attacks on existing economic privilege for later. Some attacks are directed against certain practices by which business deviously manipulates an entire class for its own economic advantage. He describes how merchants and manufacturers play upon the credulity of the countryside to gain public support for higher tariffs and other restrictions on imports. Smith refers to these importunings, aimed at persuading the rural gentry that trade restrictions benefit the countryside, as the "clamour and sophistry of manufacturers and traders."[30] Merchants and manufacturers collect together into towns, and Smith feels that this produces an "exclusive corporation spirit" among them.[31] The country gentleman, in contrast, has less contact with his counterparts and is "the least subject to the wretched spirit of monopoly."[32] He has a more generous and open nature, and the town class, knowing this, plays upon his openness to persuade him "to give up both his own interest and that of the public."[33] The country gentleman, not seeing through the sophisticated arguments of the town class, will be led to believe that market restrictions actually are to his own benefit. But when he goes to market he will have to pay higher prices for manufactured goods. To buy what one wants at the lowest possible price is to Smith a "proposition so very manifest, that it seems ridiculous to take any pains to prove it." But, sadly, "the interested sophistry of merchants and manufacturers" has called it into question and has "confounded the common sense of mankind."[34]

A second kind of manipulation by business is directed toward the laboring classes. When proposals to reduce trade restrictions and to make markets more open are brought before Parliament, employers act to "enflame their workmen, to attack with violence and outrage the proposers of any such regulation"; "like an overgrown standing army, they [the workmen] have become formidable to the government, and upon many occasions intimidate the legislature." On the other hand, when a member of Parliament supports special privileges for domestic manufacture, he "is sure to acquire not only the reputation of understanding trade, but great popularity and influence." But, if he opposes business and its labor pawns, neither "the highest rank, nor the greatest public services, can protect him from the most infamous abuse and detraction . . . nor sometimes from real danger, arising from the insolent outrage of furious and disappointed monopolists."[35] Business enlists labor's fear of foreign competition in support of its dubious goals and, by doing so, adds the threat of violence to its weapons against free markets. Smith also adds, in another place, that "Masters are always and every where in a sort of tacit, but constant and uniform combination, not to raise the wages of labour above their actual rate."[36] As businessmen conspire against their workers, they artfully manage the workers for their own political ends.

Although Smith's spirits become depressed as he faces such powerful opposition to free trade, he does occasionally see some slight encouragement when reviewing the character of man. Returning to the idea of man's intense motivation to trade and to better his condition, Smith feels that this drive is "capable of preventing and correcting, in many respects, the bad effects of a political economy, in some degree both partial and oppressive,"[37] and that it is "frequently powerful enough to maintain the natural progress of things toward improvement."[38] Perhaps the almost animal-like drive to trade will overcome some of the obstacles to free markets and the material improvement of nations.

But when Smith returns to the scene of government his spirits sink once again. To Smith, government should be the seat of national greatness and prestige; it should concern itself with the high activities of administering justice and promoting the public welfare. Government, in all of its majesty, should reign with wise deliberation high above the transient cross-currents of interest and personality below. While Smith feels deeply for this ideal of government, he knows that sordid political and economic ambitions stand in the way of its realization. He describes how, for example, the official policy of the British government favors imports of Portuguese wine over the wines of France, the argument being that Portugal is a better customer of Britain than France, so Portuguese products should be favored over French. Such reasoning, to Smith, is worthy only of lowliest tradesmen, those "who make it a rule to employ chiefly their own customers." It is one thing to have decisions of state influenced by the great captains of commerce, who at least are aware of the importance of buying in the cheapest market, but to have them influenced by the benighted notions of tradesmen is too much for Smith. He concludes that the government has fallen so low that "The sneaking arts of underling tradesmen are thus erected into political maxims for the conduct of a great empire." Such discrimination between nations sometimes becomes a source of friction leading to war. "The capricious ambition of kings and ministers has not . . . been more fatal to the repose of Europe, than the impertinent jealousy of merchants and manufacturers. The violence and injustice of the rulers of mankind is an ancient evil. . . . But the mean rapacity and monopolizing of spirit of merchants and manufacturers, who neither are, nor ought to be, the rulers of mankind," should, at least, be prevented from disturbing the peace of nations.[39]

Those who first voiced the maxim of protection "were by no means such fools as they who believed it."[40] Inventors of false doctrines are bad enough; others who believe the doctrines are worse.

Smith's sharp attacks on the government continue as he directs his attention toward the economic policies of Parliament and the king toward the colonies. These policies have concentrated most of the external trade of the colonies into British hands, forcing the trade into unnatural channels and causing the growth of imbalances in the British economy. The limited supply of capital at home, for example, has been abnormally drawn into colonial trade because of the high returns arising from its protected state. This has reduced the supply of domestic capital and has acted to impede the growth of domestic British industry. Smith likens the colonies to the abnormally large growth of one organ in the body politic, the organ having been forced beyond its normal and healthy size by the stimulative effects of protection.[41] He makes a contemptuous comparison between what a great colonial empire should be and what the British empire actually is. He relates how the American colonies were founded by those who were "uneasy at home" and how they developed into thriving and prosperous communities growing on freedom of trade. But soon the shopkeepers and traders of England, growing jealous of this freedom, asked Parliament to grant a monopoly of this trade for their benefit or, as Smith puts it, "they petitioned the parliament that the cultivators of America might for the future be confined to their shop."[42] And so the Navigation Acts were imposed on the colonies, for which Smith reserves his sharpest scorn.

> To found a great empire for the sole purpose of raising up a people of customers, may at first sight appear a project fit only for a nation of shopkeepers. It is, however, a project altogether unfit for a nation of shopkeepers; but extremely fit for a nation whose government is influenced by shopkeepers.[43]

The obstacles thrown in the way of Smith's ideal of the free market by business, labor, and government are, indeed, great, but there is another and even greater obstacle. While this last obstacle will not in and of itself impede economic growth, it may very well reduce the quality of life during this growth. It is the stultifying effect on the mind of the worker produced by excessive specialization. Smith is well aware that concentrating on one narrow job becomes boring but he also knows that, in time, it dulls the senses of the worker. If overly repetitive labor is necessary to raise the material welfare of mankind and, at the same time, it destroys the inner balance of the worker, then what price economic growth? The answer is, obviously, too high a price. This is, perhaps, the greatest challenge to Smith's goal of economic development because it strikes directly at the heart of the principle propelling the development. The detrimental effects of the division of labor on the mind of the worker did not occur to the social theorists of specialization we studied in Chapter 7. But Smith's sense of realism will not allow him to consider only the material benefits of the principle. It also forces him to examine all sides, including the impact on the personality of the worker. Smith does not temper or compromise as he draws in severe outline these bad effects of the division of labor. He warns that, after a day of labor at simple manual operations, the worker no longer has any "occasion to exert his under-standing." The torpor of his mind, induced by dulling repetitive labor, deadens his feelings, and his intellectual and social sensitivities are re-duced to low levels. He "generally becomes as stupid and ignorant as it is possible for a human creature to become." As the manual dexterity of the worker increases, his imagination shrinks, and the dexterity of his mind deteriorates.[44]

Smith believes, however, that there is an answer. These effects of the division of labor can, he thinks, be largely offset by education, if govern-ment will expand educational opportunities for the working population. If the worker's mental horizons were widened, the constricting effects of dulling labor would be neutralized in his mind and the balance of his imagination would be retained. Smith suggests programs of reading, writing, and accounting to be supplemental with gymnastic exercises, because he is also concerned that repetitive labor weakens the martial virtues. A beneficial side effect of increased education would be to make workers more orderly and respectable, thus rendering them less suscepti-ble to the "delusions of enthusiasm and superstition." It would also make them "more capable of seeing through, the interested complaints of faction and sedition."[45]

In his espousal of education as a cure for the personal problems arising from the division of labor, Smith leaves a large and important question unanswered. If education opens up the mind and spreads out the in-terests of the individual, will the individual then be willing to undergo the constricting pressures of specialized labor? Can the division of labor continue to advance in the face of widening education and the new mental attitudes and values it creates? If one takes the mind out of the factory and shows it new worlds, will the mind allow the body to go back to the factory? Smith does not really address himself to this problem. Perhaps he thought the constant drive for material betterment in the individual would carry the day and that, somehow, the best of both worlds, of productive effi-ciency and of mental ability, could be achieved. But he does not say how.

It is clear that Smith saw no easy road to the realization of the free-market system. He was too much of a realist to think otherwise. We will never really know whether he believed that the emotional drive to trade would be powerful enough in the long run to overcome the many entrenched obstacles to market freedom. His identification of these obstacles is the most comprehensive, and his attack on them the most incisive, of his century or, for that matter, of modern times. Josiah Tucker's outraged cries against monopoly fade in comparison. But when we come to the end of *The Wealth of Nations* we are filled with uncertainty. We have seen arguments that free markets *will* come about and that free markets *should* come about, some arguments claiming the inevitability of such markets and others revealing their rationality. But none of these arguments resolves clearly what Smith actually felt about the *possibility* of free markets. After reviewing his description of the massed opposition of government, business, and labor to market freedom and of the less than desirable effects of specialization on the worker, we would have to conjecture that he probably thought they were not possible. As Smith himself wrote: "To expect, indeed, that the freedom of trade should ever be entirely restored in Great Britain, is as absurd as to expect that an Oceana or Utopia should ever be established in it."[46]

Smith's empiricism led him to attempt an economic solution to the problem of self-interest and the social welfare but it also made him aware that perhaps the world was not ready for his solution. The soul of modern economic man was not to find an easy and safe refuge in the mind of Adam Smith.

Epilogue

In 1818 the Swiss-born historian and writer on economic subjects, J. C. L. Simonde de Sismondi (1773–1842), visited England. The British economy was suffering a severe slump in the aftermath of the Napoleonic Wars. The abnormal prosperity of the war period had been followed by depressed markets leading to sharp deflation. Employers cut wages, hours, and employment in an attempt to cope with the weakened economy. Poverty and hunger were spreading through the land and workers attacked machines, thinking them the cause of their lost jobs. Radicals agitated for parliamentary reorganization to deal with the crisis.

Sismondi was shocked by the conditions he saw, but more than that, he was appalled by the economic thinking and policies of the ruling classes concerning the depression. According to the new science of political economy, widely subscribed to by those in power, government should assume a neutral posture concerning the depression and let the forces of the free market work themselves out because any outside interference with wages and prices, or any attempt to liberalize relief for the destitute and unemployed, was bound to make matters worse. According to the new doctrines, economic life was controlled by laws and tendencies so powerful that government could do little or nothing to alter their operation or even deflect their course. Any attempts to do so would fail and then rebound to the detriment of all. Sismondi reacted strongly to this official policy of doing nothing in the face of great need, and called for strong action by the British government to alleviate the depressed conditions. He condemned the current policy of inaction, asserting that "there is only one step from this doctrine to denying the existence of evil."[1]

To make matters worse, this new political economy also saw the long-term future threatened by a permanent state of penury and starvation. Even if the economy could struggle back to a level of prosperity through its own short-term powers of recuperation, this would only be temporary because economic laws operating over a longer time-span would finally defeat this revival. Again, nothing could be done to alter or deflect

126

significantly the operation of these long-term laws leading to a state of destitution.

Adam Smith, as we have seen, inherited optimistic attitudes about the relation between self-interest and the public welfare from his predecessors in philosophy, and he translated their theories about self-interest into a new language, economics. Fully aware of the fallability of man in general and of men in government and business in particular, Smith entertained reservations about the ability of business and government to implement free markets, which he saw as a necessity to insure that self-interest served the public welfare. His economic system was, nevertheless, optimistic on balance as he argued that man's future held definite possibilities for permanent material and social improvement. Smith's economic horizon was not blocked by impenetrable barriers to a better future because he believed that man was capable of making himself largely what he wished, if only he could be made to see through the devious designs of those who would restrict markets.

Now, however, in post-Napoleonic Britain a newer political economy pointed not to the possibility of economic improvement through self-interest operating in a system of free markets but to the inevitability of economic deterioration dictated by inexorable law. What had brought an end to the long tradition of optimism about self-interest? The answer is Ricardian economics—iron principles based upon the scourging law of diminishing returns.

David Ricardo was born in London in 1772. He received his early education in a common school and at the age of eleven was sent by his father, a stockbroker, to Holland for further schooling and to become acquainted with the country with which his father had important financial business. It is evident that young Ricardo was being prepared to follow in the family business and, at the age of fourteen, his father gave him serious responsibilities in handling his affairs on the Stock Exchange. Later, he broke with his father but was offered aid by business friends and associates in the City; in a short time he made considerable profits on the stock market and began to enjoy financial independence. In later years he accumulated great wealth acting as underwriter for loans to the British government during the Napoleonic Wars. He died in 1823.

Ricardo did not have an education in the classics. His intellectual interests as a young man turned toward scientific subjects such as chemistry, geology, mineralogy, and that purest of sciences, mathematics. When in later life his attention turned to economics, his approach seems to have been influenced by this earlier interest in the sciences, for a historical or philosophical view toward economic problems is almost completely lacking in his work. His approach to economics is selective, as he concentrates on one problem at a time to the exclusion of all else. His major work, *The*

Principles of Political Economy and Taxation (1817), is composed of many short but dense chapters, each argued with great precision in order to reach only a limited objective. It is a handbook of tactics for the reasoner in economics, and Ricardo's singleness of purpose, his attention to detail, proved so impressive and convincing that his thought made a great impact on the established opinion of his day.

Ricardo's method in economics is that of pure theory. As each problem is taken up it is surrounded by a set of hypothetical conditions which are almost always introduced by the words "if" or "suppose," words that occur hundreds of times in the book. From these assumed conditions he then constructs ordered chains of economic cause and effect, often long and intricate ones, until he reaches his final conclusion about the problem. The deductive method is everything; cold logic is all.

The substance of Ricardian economics rests on two premises: a rapid and continuous growth in population and, at the same time, a slowing growth in agricultural production. The Malthusian specter of an inevitable press of population on the food supply is never long out of sight for Ricardo. Economic growth, he argued, must halt because the resources required to sustain it are becoming ever more difficult to obtain. As a growing population demands more food and necessities, farmers will attempt to increase their output but, due to the fact that all land is not of equal quality, they will have to resort to less fertile acres and this will, in turn, reduce the size of the increments to their production. Eventually, total farm output must fall behind the requirements of increasing population as niggardly nature gradually defeats man in his age-old struggle to escape poverty. Here is a law based upon physical fact, the law of diminishing returns, making all positive speculations about the future of man beside the point.

And this is not all. As the battle against the stringencies of nature intensifies, friction and potential for conflict will grow among the classes composing society. The incomes accruing to the three economic classes—landowners, laborers, and capitalists—are all ultimately derived from the national income flowing from the production and sale of the products and services of society. Incomes of the three classes are derived from a finite pool of funds and, consequently, each category of income can be increased only at the expense of one or both of the others. The amount drained from the pool of national income by the landowning class, or by rent, depends upon the current degree of land scarcity and is similar to the exaction of a monopolist. It is not a payment made for an active participation in production by the landowner himself but rests simply on the fact that he controls a scarce resource for which he can charge whatever the traffic will bear. The remainder of the funds in the pool of national income flows initially to the capitalist, and part will be paid out by him as wages to labor while he retains the rest for himself as profit. So each of these latter two portions of income, wages and profits, is also paid out at the expense of the other. Ricardo returns to this point again and again as he summarizes it with the rhetorical question: "Can any point be more clearly established than that profits must fall with a rise in wages?"[2] Very simply, as the employer pays more for wages, the less remains for his profit, and vice versa.

In the long run several things occur to increase friction in this three-way struggle for the wealth of a nation. Because of the increasing scarcity of land in the face of the press of population, the landowner will demand and receive a larger and larger portion of the national income. He will grow wealthier both in absolute and relative terms compared to the worker and capitalist. Just how much of the residue of national income, after the landowner has taken his share, will go to the worker and to the capitalist, Ricardo does not make clear. At one point he argues that the capitalist will fall behind the worker in claiming the residue because higher and higher wages must be paid in order to meet the higher cost of necessities caused by the increasing difficulty of extracting more output from the land.[3] Subsistence for the worker will cost more, so the employer must pay higher wages if he is to obtain a labor supply. Thus, the capitalist will fall behind labor in the division of the residue of national income.

Later, Ricardo points toward another possibility. As the capitalist faces the challenge of having to pay higher and higher wages, he will be forced to direct more of his funds into plant and equipment in an attempt to raise labor productivity so that he will be able to pay the higher wages. Or, alternatively, he will strive to meet the higher wages by replacing some of his work force with machines. As a result he will direct more of his funds into fixed capital and retain less as circulating or liquid capital, the form of capital from which wages are paid. As that portion of the employer's funds from which wages can be paid declines, fewer jobs will be made available and unemployment will rise. Consequently, in this case, the laborer will suffer more than the capitalist in this final apportioning of the residue of national income.[4]

Ricardo never completely settles this question of which—labor or capital—will win out in the division of the income. In any event, the individual interests of these two classes remain unalterably opposed, while their common interest falls increasingly under the power of the landlord. In sum, Ricardo's economics foresees the eventual destitution of the majority of the population, and, on the way to this grim end, he predicts intensifying social divisions and potential for class conflict.

Ricardo based his economics on what he conceived to be basic and immutable forces regulating the life of man and the operations of nature. Laws of human passion increase human reproduction while laws of agronomy decrease the size of the increments to agricultural production. In this context one stares at questions concerning the very survival of large parts of the human race. It is, therefore, not surprising that Ricardo largely ignored lesser questions. The problem of self-interest and the public welfare, so central to the economics of Adam Smith, pales into insignificance when viewed against the crisis economics of Ricardo. If mankind is facing a battle for its very future here on earth, then speculations about self-interest would seem rather poor preparation for what promises to be an ultimate physical ordeal. Although Ricardo recognized self-interest as the prime mover in modern economic man, he did not worry about its finer meanings, implications, or shadings in terms of social theory. He took the drive of self-interest for granted, not asking, as eighteenth-century minds did, how or why it arises in the human soul, and not tracing its ultimate meanings. Man must suffer the operations of natural law; *that* is the subject of utmost importance. Over a century of thought and intense interest about the higher meanings of self-interest comes to an end with Ricardo as he removes man and his motives from their central position in economics and replaces them with relentless economic law. Man and his many-sided nature are no longer seen as the source of economic activity, as Ricardo makes of man simply a thing to be ground down by the faceless powers of nature.

We end on a note of paradox. Early British political economy, with its emphasis on the motives and actions of the individual, gained its distinct flavor and character from the climate of ideas created by our philosophers of self-interest. Adam Smith's economics is a culmination of the influence of these thinkers, of minds who had studied in great detail the problem of self-interest during the century preceeding the publication of *The Wealth of Nations*. Smith inherited his world view from a climate of philosophical liberalism, translated this world view and its conclusions concerning the individual into economic terms, and, in doing so, constructed a material proof that self-interest operating in the real world of production and trade could, indeed, be made to serve the public welfare. In doing this Smith and his philosophical predecessors created a current of optimism that dominated the world of ideas until the end of the eighteenth century. These positive feelings about man, socially and materially, rested on the belief that while man was giving expression to his most natural inner motives, which were inbred in him for his own survival, he was, at the same time, also serving the larger interest of society. Happily, man could act as his natural self and also be a moral being. This viewpoint, as translated into the economic terms of free markets, was to provide an inspiration for the coming industrialism of the West.

The essential features of industrialism might be defined in several ways, but one of the most striking characteristics of this movement was the completely unprecedented number of people who felt themselves free to produce new products, to try out radically new methods of production, and to seek new employments. It was a system offering much greater freedom of movement than in the past—freedom to seek new jobs and new places to live. During no time in history had so many people moved to so many new jobs in so many new places. The Western economies were transformed as the modern entrepreneur, by heroic efforts, shifted the bulk of national resources out of traditional employments and into new operations which concentrated on specific products made by highly specialized labor. Smith's emphasis on economic individualism and the division of labor could hardly have been more fully realized. This great transformation was marred by human suffering and severe problems of adjustment but it did eventually raise the level of living in the West to unprecedented heights. For the first time in history a small but significant part of the human race succeeded in constructing an economic system capable of generating large and continuing economic surpluses. Smith's vision of improved material conditions for man had been clearly achieved and, in spite of his pessimism about the realizing of free markets, largely on the terms he foresaw.

But the interesting point is that Smith's vision of material betterment was, originally, inspired by the speculation of some of the more noneconomic minds in the history of ideas, the minds we studied in the earlier chapters. Could anything, for example, seem farther apart than the fine literary tracings of a Shaftesbury or a Pope about the nature of self-interest and the raw and massive mountains of iron, sugar, shoes, and so much more produced by the industrial revolution? Yet the open and liberal interpretation of the motives of the individual by a Shaftesbury helped to create a mental climate which was, in turn, to direct Smith toward a similar interpretation of the actions of the individual in economic life. Ideas can have results, material ones of the greatest magnitude.

And to make the paradox more complete, Ricardo, that hard realist who came up through practical contacts in business and finance, who lived in the vortex of the industrial revolution, failed to appreciate adequately the impact of the rising productivity of the machines and men all around him. His excessive concentration on economic categories to the exclusion of all else made him unaware of the great and open-ended potential of industrial production to reduce poverty. There is far more in economic reality than the selective categories imposed on it by the minds of economists.

Notes

CHAPTER 1

1. Arthur Lovejoy, *The Great Chain of Being* (New York: Harper & Brothers, 1960), p. 7.
2. Ibid., p. 10.
3. Ibid., p. 15.
4. Jacob Viner, *Studies in the Theory of International Trade* (New York: Harper & Brothers, 1937), p. 91.
5. Jacob Viner, "The Intellectual History of Laissez-Faire," Henry Simons Lecture, University of Chicago Law School, November 18, 1959; published as pamphlet by University of Chicago Law School (1961), p. 58.
6. R. H. Tawney, *Religion and the Rise of Capitalism* (New York: New American Library of World Literature, 1952), p. 205.

CHAPTER 2

1. Although I am not directly concerned with the work of writers on business subjects, a number of these writers were already exploring the larger, economy-wide effects of trade. This is the period of mercantilism and the concern of these writers with national economic power is very evident.
2. Joseph Addison and Richard Steele, *The Spectator*, ed. Gregory Smith, 4 vols. (London: J. M. Dent and Sons, 1967), 1:8.
3. Ibid., 4:229.
4. Ibid., 2:17.
5. Ibid., p. 18.
6. Ibid., p. 19.
7. Ibid.
8. Ibid., 1:212.
9. Ibid., p. 213.
10. Ibid., p. 214.
11. Daniel Defoe, *A Plan of the English Commerce*, 2d ed. (New York: Augustus M. Kelley, 1967), pp. 6–9.
12. Ibid., p. 9.
13. Ibid., pp. 10–11.
14. Ibid., p. 32.
15. Ibid., p. 69.

16. Ibid., p. 68.

17. Ibid., p. 100.

18. Edward Young, *The Poetical Works*, 2 vols. (reprint of Aldine edition; Westport, Conn.: Greenwood Press, 1970), 2:342.

19. Ibid., p. 346.

20. Ibid., p. 357.

21. Ibid., p. 358.

22. William Cowper, *Poetical Works*, ed. H. S. Milford (London: Oxford University Press, 1967), p. 76.

23. Ibid., p. 78.

24. Ibid.

25. *Josiah Tucker: A Selection of His Economic and Political Writings* (New York: Columbia University Press, 1931), p. 58.

26. Ibid.

27. Ibid., p. 60.

28. Ibid., p. 92.

29. Ibid., p. 135.

30. Ibid., pp. 159, 166, 178, 179.

31. Adam Smith, *The Wealth of Nations*, ed. Edwin Cannan (New York: Random House, 1937), p. 128.

32. Ibid.; see also p. 429.

33. Ibid., p. 438.

34. Ibid., p. 460.

35. Ibid., p. 461.

36. Ibid., pp. 734–35; Adam Ferguson, *An Essay on the History of Civil Society* (1767; Edinburgh: Edinburgh University Press, 1966), pp. 181–83; William C. Lehmann, *John Millar of Glasgow* (Cambridge: Cambridge University Press, 1960), pp. 379–82.

37. William Godwin, *Political Justice*, ed. F. E. L. Priestley, 3d. ed., 3 vols. (Toronto: University of Toronto Press, 1969), 2:513.

38. Ibid., p. 514.

39. Ibid., p. 309–10.

40. Because I am confining my attention mainly to those writers with a literary background, I will avoid the many attacks made on economic man and his system by the "scientific" critics of capitalism, the socialists and others. The humanistic background of our literary-based critics provides deeper insights into the inner motives of economic man than does the mechanistic or scientist approach taken by many of these critics.

41. Thomas Carlyle, *Past and Present* (1843; London: Oxford University Press, 1960), p. 276.

42. Ibid., p. 31.

43. Ibid., p. 195.

44. Ibid., p. 59.

45. Carlyle, "The Present Time" (1850), *Latter-Day Pamphlets* (New York: AMS Press, 1969), p. 21.

46. Ibid., p. 45.

47. Carlyle, "Burns" (1828), *Scottish and Other Miscellanies*, (London: J. M. Dent and Sons, 1946), p. 28.

48. Carlyle, "Chartism" (1839), *English and Other Critical Essays* (London: J. M. Dent and Sons, 1950), p. 227.

49. Ibid., p. 228. Interestingly, Carlyle anticipates Keynes's attack on the "long run" by almost a century.

50. Carlyle, "Signs of the Times" (1829), *Scottish and Other Miscellanies*, p. 234.

51. Carlyle, *Past and Present*, p. 29.

52. Ibid., p. 152.

53. Ibid., p. 159.

54. Carlyle, "The Present Time," *Latter-Day Pamphlets*, p. 18.

55. Carlyle, "Inaugural Address at Edinburgh" (1866), *Scottish and Other Miscellanies*, p. 167.

56. Carlyle, "Chartism," *English and Other Critical Essays*, p. 185.

57. John Ruskin, *Unto This Last*, (1862; New York: John W. Lovell Co., n.d.), pp. 18–19.

58. Ibid., p. 69.

59. Ibid., p. 77.

60. Ruskin, *Crown of Wild Olive* (1866; New York: John W. Lovell Co., n.d.), p. 60.

61. Ruskin, *Unto This Last*, p. 14.

62. Ruskin, *Munera Pulveris* (1863; New York: John W. Lovell Co., n.d.), p. 101.

63. Ibid., p. 34.

64. Ruskin, *Unto This Last*, p. 87.

65. Ruskin, *Crown of Wild Olive*, p. 21.

66. Ruskin, *Munera Pulveris*, p. 127n.

CHAPTER 3

1. For various comments on this point, see: Margaret Jacob, *The Newtonians and the English Revolution, 1689–1720* (Ithaca, N.Y.: Cornell University Press, 1976), p. 56; C. H. Wilson, "Trade, Society, and the State," *Cambridge Economic History of Europe*, ed. E. E. Rich and C. H. Wilson (Cambridge: Cambridge University Press, 1967), 4:540–41; J. A. W. Gunn, *Politics and the Public Interest in the Seventeenth Century* (London: Routledge & Kegan Paul, 1969), pp. 266, 277; R. F. Jones, *Ancients and Moderns*, 2d ed. (Berkeley and Los Angeles: University of California Press, 1965), p. 88; H. M. Robertson, *Aspects of the Rise of Economic Individualism* (Cambridge: Cambridge University Press, 1933), p. 17. For comments on the modernity of Hobbes, see John Bowle, *Hobbes and His Critics* (London: Jonathan Cape, 1951), pp. 52–53.

2. Thomas Hobbes, *De Cive*, ed. S. P. Lamprecht (New York: Appleton-Century-Crofts, 1949), p. 16.

3. Hobbes, *Leviathan* (London: J. M. Dent & Sons, 1962), p. 391.

4. Hobbes also associates the process of reasoning with addition and subtraction. Ibid., p. 18.

5. Ibid., pp. 1 and 30 respectively.

135

6. Ibid., p. 4.
7. Hobbes, "Human Nature" (1650), *The English Works of Thomas Hobbes,* ed. Sir William Molesworth, 11 vols. (London: John Bohn, 1839–45), 4:52–53. Certain writers feel that Hobbes's basic conception of man was formed prior to his knowledge of modern science. See Leo Strauss, *The Political Philosophy of Hobbes,* trans. E. M. Sinclair (Chicago: University of Chicago Press, 1963), pp. ix–xi.
8. Hobbes, *Leviathan,* p. 63.
9. Ibid., p. 64.
10. Ibid.
11. Ibid., p. 65.
12. Ibid., p. 67.
13. Hobbes, *De Corpore Politico* (1650), *English Works,* 4:85.
14. Ibid., p. 84.
15. Hobbes, *Leviathan,* p. 66.
16. Ibid., p. 87.
17. Ibid., p. 131.
18. Ibid., p. 170.
19. Hobbes, *De Corpore Politico, English Works,* 4:164.
20. Hobbes, Leviathan, p. 177.
21. Hobbes, *De Corpore Politico, English Works,* 4:101.
22. Hobbes, *De Cive,* p. 22.
23. Ibid., p. 24.
24. Ibid.
25. Ibid.

CHAPTER 4

1. For a check list of works attacking Hobbes, see Samuel Mintz, *The Hunting of Leviathan* (Cambridge: Cambridge University Press, 1962), pp. 157–60.
2. Richard Cumberland, *A Treatise of the Laws of Nature,* trans. John Maxwell (London: 1727), p. 35.
3. Ibid., p. 36.
4. Ibid.
5. Ibid., p. 14
6. Ibid.
7. Ibid., p. 13.
8. Ibid., p. 15.
9. Ibid., p. 108.
10. Ibid., p. 31.
11. Ibid., p. 70.
12. Ibid., p. 118.
13. Ibid., p. 119.
14. Ibid., p. 41
15. Ibid., p. 35.
16. Ibid., pp. 45, 46, 56, 62, 197. Cumberland does back off somewhat and admits in one place that morality is, perhaps, not as exact a science as mathematics (p. 185).
17. Ibid., p. 120. John Maxwell, in a footnote to this statement, feels the source

of Cumberland's idea of plenitude is in the work of Descartes. He is somewhat concerned about Cumberland's use of the idea because he claims it was later disproved by Newton. But, on balance, Maxwell feels no great harm is done to Cumberland's system by the use of the idea of plenitude.

18. Ibid., p. 120.
19. Ibid., p. 113; see also pp. 115, 118.
20. Ibid., p. 46n.
21. Ibid., p. 215.
22. Ibid., p. 106.
23. Ibid., p. 272.
24. Ibid., p. 236.
25. Ibid., p. 332.
26. Ibid., p. 70.
27. Ibid., p. 114.
28. Ibid., p. 236.
29. Ibid., p. 296.
30. Ibid., p. 297.
31. Ibid., p. 306. Cumberland appears to anticipate by some two hundred years the famous Pareto optimum.
32. Ibid., p. 39.
33. Ibid., p. 64.
34. Ibid., p. 65.
35. Ibid., p. 314.
36. Ibid., p. 324.
37. Arthur O. Lovejoy, *The Great Chain of Being* (New York: Harper & Brothers, 1960), p. 52. There is considerable literature on the naturalism of the period. For a few examples: Carl L. Becker, *The Heavenly City of the Eighteenth-Century Philosophers* (New Haven: Yale University Press, 1959); Robert H. Hurlbutt, *Hume, Newton, and the Design Argument* (Lincoln: University of Nebraska Press, 1965); Basil Willey, *The Eighteenth Century Background* (Boston: Beacon Press, 1961).
38. Ibid., pp. 50, 51.
39. Ibid., p. 52.
40. Ibid., p. 54.
41. Ibid., p. 181.
42. Ibid., p. 128.
43. Ibid., p. 111.
44. At least one major figure in the study of ideas, Jacob Viner, discerned an influence of Cumberland on Smith. See Viner's *The Role of Providence in the Social Order* (Philadelphia: American Philosophical Society, 1972), p. 65.

CHAPTER 5
1. Shaftesbury, *The Life, Unpublished Letters, and Philosophical Regimen*, ed. Benjamin Rand (New York: Macmillan, 1900), p. 403.
2. Ibid.
3. Ibid., p. 404.
4. Ibid., p. 416.

5. Shaftesbury, *Characteristics of Men, Manners, Opinions, Times*, ed. John M. Robertson, 2 vols. in 1 (Indianapolis & New York: Bobbs-Merrill, 1964), 2:4–5.

6. Ibid., 2:5.

7. Ibid., 1:189.

8. Ibid., 1:215.

9. Ibid., 1:240–41.

10. Ibid., 2:122.

11. Ibid., 2:113.

12. Ibid., 2:64.

13. Ibid., 2:65.

14. Ibid., 2:93.

15. Ibid., 1:193.

16. Ibid., 1:196.

17. Ibid., 1:79.

18. Ibid., 1:77.

19. Ibid., 1:81.

20. Ibid., 1:248.

21. Ibid., 1:243.

22. Ibid., 1:74.

23. Ibid., 1:75.

24. Ibid., 1:314.

25. Ibid., 1:284.

26. Ibid., 1:291.

27. Ibid., 1:289.

28. Ibid., 1:337.

29. Ibid., 1:282.

30. Ibid., 1:336.

31. Ibid., 1:314.

32. Ibid., 2:28.

33. Ibid., 1:78.

34. Ibid., 1:314.

35. Ibid., 1:45–46.

36. Joseph Butler, *Sermons*, in L. A. Selby-Bigge, ed., *British Moralists*, 2 vols. (New York: Dover Publications, 1965), 1:181.

37. Ibid., 1:209.

38. Ibid., 1:184.

39. Ibid., 1:197.

40. Ibid., 1:201.

41. Ibid., 1:220.

42. Ibid., 1:193.

43. Ibid.

44. Ibid., 1:197.

45. Ibid., 1:194.

46. Ibid., 1:199.

47. Ibid., 1:201.

48. Ibid., 1:238.

49. Ibid., 1:239.

50. Alexander Pope, *The Poetical Works*, ed. Adolphus William Ward (New York: Thomas Y. Crowell, 1896), p. 194.
51. Ibid., p. 195.
52. Ibid., p. 198.
53. Ibid., p. 203.
54. Ibid., pp. 203–4.
55. Ibid., p. 204.
56. Ibid., p. 204.
57. Ibid., p. 206.
58. Ibid., p. 217.
59. Ibid., p. 218.

CHAPTER 6

1. Adam Smith, "The History of the Ancient Logics and Metaphysics," *Works of Adam Smith*, 5 vols. (reprint of 1811–12 ed.; Aalen: Otto Zeller, 1963), 5:232.
2. For a short review of some of these writers, see Michael Macklem, *The Anatomy of the World* (Minneapolis: University of Minnesota Press, 1958), app. 2.
3. David Hume, *A Treatise of Human Nature*, 2 vols. (London: J. M. Dent & Sons, 1959), 1:21.
4. Ibid., p. 159.
5. [Peter Paxton], *Civil Polity, A Treatise Concerning the Nature of Government* (London: 1703), p. 35. Paxton is an early user of a term common in his period and one which, eventually, will find its way into the American Declaration of Independence: "pursuit of happiness."
6. Ibid., p. 7.
7. Ibid.
8. Ibid., p. 30.
9. Ibid., p. 31.
10. Ibid., p. 35.
11. L. A. Selby-Bigge, ed., *British Moralists*, 2 vols. (New York: Dover Publications, 1965), 1:74.
12. Ibid., p. 82.
13. Ibid., p. 130.
14. Ibid., p. 164.
15. Ibid.
16. Francis Hutcheson, *A System of Moral Philosophy*, 2 vols. (London: A. Foulis, 1755), 2:318–20.
17. *Works of Lord Bolingbroke*, 4 vols. (reprint of 1844 ed.; New York: Augustus M. Kelley, 1967), 4:160.
18. Ibid., p. 147.
19. Ibid., p. 165.
20. Ibid., p. 363. For sources of the term "moral gravitation," see A. D. McKillop, *The Background of Thomson's Seasons* (Minneapolis: University of Minnesota Press, 1942), p. 36.
21. The review contains some of the better examples of Johnson's writing techniques, but our purpose here is not to examine his literary skills. For the review, see R. B. Schwartz, *Samuel Johnson and the Problem of Evil* (Madison:

University of Wisconsin Press, 1975), app. 3; or, for the original, *The Literary Magazine* (London), 2 (1757).

22. *The Works of Soame Jenyns*, 4 vols. (reprint of 1790 ed., Westmead, Eng.: Gregg International Publishers, 1969), 3:43–44.

23. Ibid., p. 44.

24. Ibid., pp. 45–46.

25. Ibid., p. 43.

26. Ibid., p. 62.

27. Ibid., p. 49.

28. Ibid., p. 120.

29. Ibid., p. 122.

30. Ibid., p. 123.

31. Ibid., p. 85.

32. Ibid., p. 234.

33. Ibid., pp. 234–35.

34. Ibid., p. 238.

35. Ibid., pp. 238–39.

36. Ibid., p. 239.

37. Ibid., pp. 240–41.

38. Ibid., p. 244.

39. *Works of Bolingbroke*, 4:338.

40. Quoted in Lovejoy, *Chain of Being*, p. 210.

41. E. M. W. Tillyard, *The Elizabethan World Picture* (New York: Random House, n.d.), p. 26.

CHAPTER 7

1. Basil Willey, *The English Moralists* (Garden City, N.Y.: Doubleday, 1967), p. 210.

2. Bernard Mandeville, *Fable of the Bees*, ed. F. B. Kaye, 2 vols. (Oxford: The Clarendon Press, 1957), 2:284.

3. Robert Jacques Turgot, *Reflections on the Formation and Distribution of Riches* (New York: Augustus M. Kelley, 1963), p. 42.

4. David Hume, *A Treatise of Human Nature*, ed. A. D. Lindsay, 2 vols. (London: J. M. Dent & Sons, 1956), 2:191.

5. Adam Ferguson, *An Essay on the History of Civil Society*, ed. Duncan Forbes (Edinburgh: Edinburgh University Press, 1966), pp. 180–84.

6. Addison and Steele, *The Spectator*, ed. Gregory Smith, 4 vols. (London: J. M. Dent & Sons, 1967), 2:190.

7. For this background on Derham's *Physico-Theology*, see Robert E. Schofield, *Mechanism and Materialism* (Princeton, N.J.: Princeton University Press, 1970), pp. 20–26.

8. William Derham, *Physico-Theology*, 2 vols. (London: 1798), 2:143.

9. Ibid., pp. 143–44.

10. Ibid., p. 144.

11. Ibid., p. 164.

12. From Maxwell's "Remark on Chap. 1" in Cumberland, *A Treatise of the Laws of Nature*, trans. John Maxwell (London: 1727), p. 92.

13. Ibid., p. 92.
14. Ibid., p. 92.
15. James Harris, *Three Treatises*, 2d ed. (London: 1765), p. 143.
16. Ibid., pp. 149–51.
17. Ibid., p. 152.
18. Ibid., p. 153.
19. Ibid.
20. Ibid., pp. 154–55.
21. Ibid., p. 154.
22. Ibid., p. 241.
23. Ibid., pp. 242–43.
24. Ibid., p. 244.
25. Joseph Priestley, *An Essay on the First Principles of Government*, 2d ed. (London: 1771), pp. 2–3.
26. Ibid., p. 3.
27. Ibid., p. 4.
28. Ibid., pp. 4–5.
29. Roy F. Harrod, *The Life of John Maynard Keynes*, (London: Macmillan, 1951), pp. 193–94.

CHAPTER 8

1. Horst C. Recktenwald, "An Adam Smith Renaissance *anno* 1976?," *Journal of Economic Literature* 16, no. 1 (March 1978).
2. Charles Vereker, *Eighteenth-Century Optimism* (Liverpool: Liverpool University Press, 1967), p. 108.
3. John Carswell, *The Old Cause* (London: The Cresset Press, 1954), pp. 12–14; J. G. A. Pocock, *The Machiavellian Moment* (Princeton, N.J.: Princeton University Press, 1975), p. 423.
4. Christopher Hill, *The Century of Revolution, 1603–1714* (New York: W. W. Norton, 1961), p. 4.
5. Adam Smith, "The Principles which lead and direct Philosophical Enquiries; illustrated by the History of Astronomy," *The Works of Adam Smith*, 5 vols. (Aalen: Otto Zeller, 1963), 5: sec. II, p. 65; hereafter "History of Astronomy" and *Works*, respectively.
6. Ibid., sec. I. p. 58.
7. Ibid., sec. II., p. 71.
8. Ibid., p. 73.
9. Ibid.
10. Ibid.
11. Ibid. p. 74.
12. Ibid., pp. 81–82.
13. Ibid. p. 82.
14. Ibid., p. 83.
15. Ibid.
16. Ibid., p. 84.
17. Ibid., sec. IV., p. 151.
18. Ibid., pp. 150–51.

19. Ibid., pp. 158–59.

20. Adam Smith, *The Wealth of Nations*, ed. Edwin Cannan (New York: Modern Library, 1937), p. 638.

21. Ibid.

22. Adam Smith, "History of Astronomy," *Works*, 5:221.

23. Ibid., p. 232.

24. Ibid., pp. 232–33.

25. Ibid., pp. 234–35.

26. Adam Smith, *The Theory of Moral Sentiments* (New York: Augustus M. Kelley, 1966), pt. VII, sec. II, chap. I, pp. 423–24; hereafter *Moral Sentiments*.

27. Ibid., p. 424.

28. Ibid., p. 425.

29. Ibid., pp. 425–26.

30. Ibid., sec. IV, p. 499.

31. Ibid., p. 500.

32. Adam Smith, "History of Astronomy," *Works*, 5: sec. IV, p. 175.

33. Ibid., p. 188.

34. Ibid., p. 189.

35. Ibid.

36. Walter Bagehot, *Economic Studies*, ed. R. H. Hutton (London: Longmans, Greene, 1880), p. 131.

37. Gilbert Ryle, *The Concept of Mind* (New York: Barnes & Noble, 1949), p. 8; see also pp. 16, 18–20.

38. *Moral Sentiments*, pt. II, sec. II, chap. III, p. 126.

39. Ibid., p. 128.

40. Ibid., p. 130.

41. Ibid., pp. 126–27.

42. Ibid., pt. VII, sec. II, chap. I, p. 429.

43. Ibid., pt. III, chap. I, p. 162.

44. Ibid., p. 164.

45. Ibid., pt. I, sec. I, chap. II, p. 10.

46. Ibid., pt. II, sec. II, chap. II, p. 119.

47. Ibid., pt. I, sec. I, chap. IV, p. 23.

48. Ibid., pt. II, sec. II, chap. II, p. 120.

49. Ibid., sec. I, chap. V, p. 109n.

50. Ibid., pt. III, chap. III, p. 203.

51. Ibid., chap. V, p. 236.

52. Ibid., p. 239.

53. *British Moralists*, 2 vols., ed. L. A. Selby-Bigge (New York: Dover Publications, 1965), 1:lx–lxi.

54. J. A. Farrer, *Adam Smith* (New York: G. P. Putnam's Sons, 1881), p. 25.

55. Thomas H. Huxley, *Evolution and Ethics and Other Essays* (New York and London: D. Appleton, 1929), p. 28.

CHAPTER 9

1. Edward Gibbon, *Letters of Edward Gibbon*, ed. J. E. Norton, 3 vols. (New York: Macmillan, 1956), 2:101.

2. Ibid., p. 166.

3. James Boswell, *The Life of Samuel Johnson* (New York: Modern Library, n.d.), p. 579.

4. For a discussion of this point, see Adam Smith, *The Theory of Moral Sentiments*, ed. D. D. Raphael and A. L. Macfie (Oxford: Oxford University Press, Glasgow Edition, 1976), pp. 20–25.

5. Adam Smith, *The Wealth of Nations*, ed. Edwin Cannan (New York: Modern Library, 1937), p. lvii; hereafter *WN*.

6. Ibid., p. 3.

7. Ibid., p. 13.

8. Ibid., p. 14.

9. Adam Smith, *Lectures on Justice, Police, Revenue and Arms*, ed. Edwin Cannan (1763; New York: Augustus M. Kelley, 1964), pt. II, div. II, p. 171.

10. Adam Smith, *The Theory of Moral Sentiments* (New York: Augustus M. Kelley, 1966), pt. I, sec. III, chap. II, p. 70.

11. Ibid., p. 71.

12. Ibid., p. 72.

13. Ibid., pt. IV, chap. I, p. 262.

14. Ibid., p. 263.

15. Ibid., p. 265.

16. Ibid., pp. 265–66.

17. *WN*, p. 22.

18. Ibid., p. 17.

19. Ibid., p. 29.

20. Ibid., p. 30.

21. Ibid., pp. 31–32.

22. Ibid., p. 33.

23. Ibid., pp. 47–54.

24. Ibid., p. 55.

25. Ibid., pp. 55–58.

26. Ibid., pp. 121–22.

27. Leslie Stephen, *History of English Thought in the Eighteenth Century*, 2 vols. (London: Rupert Hart-Davis, 1962), 2:270.

28. *WN*, p. 60.

29. Ibid., p. 61.

30. Ibid., p. 128.

31. Ibid., p. 429.

32. Ibid., p. 428.

33. Ibid., p. 250.

34. Ibid., p. 461.

35. Ibid., p. 438.

36. Ibid., pp. 66–67.

37. Ibid., p. 638.

38. Ibid., p. 326.

39. Ibid., p. 460.

40. Ibid., p. 461.

41. Ibid., p. 571.

42. Ibid., p. 580.
43. Ibid., p. 579.
44. Ibid., pp. 734–35.
45. Ibid., p. 740.
46. Ibid., p. 437.

Epilogue

1. J. C. L. Simonde de Sismondi, *Nouveau Principes D'Economie Politique*, 2 vols. (Paris: Delaunay, 1819), 1:395.

2. David Ricardo, *The Principles of Political Economy and Taxation* (London: J. M. Dent & Sons, 1948), p. 68.

3. Ibid., pp. 71–75.
4. Ibid., pp. 265–69.

Index

Addison, Joseph: writer of *Spectator*, 13; on trade and finance, 15
Analogy: favored by eighteenth-century thinkers, 97; used to project ideas, 98; Smith attacks misuse of, 98–99; 102–3
Aristoxenus, criticized by Smith, 98

Bagehot, Walter, criticizes Smith, 102
Bolingbroke, Lord (Henry St. John): life of, 69; on evil, 74; influence on Pope, 70; on reason and passions, 70; on self-love as gravity, 70; theodicies of, 74
Butler, Joseph (bishop of Bristol and, later, Durham): life of, 57–58; conscience controls motives, 58; on design penetrating man, 58; prefers realism in study of morals, 57; on motives respecting self and the public, 58; on quality of self-love, 59; on self-love and public interest, 59–60; anticipates Smith's "invisible hand," 60

Casuistry, Smith attacks, 101
Carlyle, Thomas, on classical economics and industrialism, 22–23
Chain of Being, described, 46, 71–72, 74, 80. *See also* Lovejoy
Continuousness, property of in nature, 47
Cooper, Anthony Ashley. *See* Shaftesbury
Cowper, William, poetry of extols trade, 17
Cumberland, Richard (bishop of Peterborough): life of, 38–39; on "benevolence," 43–44; and Cambridge Platonists, 38; on design, 41–43; sees equilibrium in nature and in society, 45; refutes Hobbes, 38–39; questions innate ideas, 40; Maxwell questions his "benevolence," 43; sees moral law derived from natural law, 40; sees morality as product of the senses, 38, 40; on nature, 40–43, 45; on plenitude, 42–43; on property rights, 45–46; on self-interest and the public welfare, 44–45; influence of on the ideas of Smith, 49

De Coverly, Sir Roger: character in *Spectator*, 14; criticizes trade and traders, 14
Defoe, Daniel: defends "Mechanicks," 15; defends trade and traders, 16
Derham, William: life of, 80; on design, 80; on division of labor, 81–82; on self-interest and the public welfare, 81; disregards trade, 81–82; variety in nature and in man, 81
Descartes, René, Smith on, 97
Design, principle of: described, 3, 46–48; Butler on, 58; Cumberland on, 41–43; Derham on, 80; difficult to apply to man, 65; difficult to prove, 65; Jenyns on, 71–72; Pope on, 61; more proof of needed, 66; Shaftesbury on, 52–54; Smith on, 97, 103
Dickens, Charles: divides soul of economic man in two, 24; attacks industrialism, 24
Diminishing returns, principle of, in Ricardian economics, 127–28

Economic man: Dickens's attack on, 24; diversity of his works and character, 16; Carlyle attacks, 22–23; Cowper admires, 17; De Coverly criticizes, 14; Defoe defends, 15–16; Freeport defends, 14; Ruskin attacks, 25; self-interest his soul, 11, 26–27; Smith uneasy about, 125; Young admires, 16

145

Economics, classical: as answer to problem in philosophy, 2, 5; and principle of diminishing returns, 21, 127–28; its advocacy of economic man, 21; establishment of, 21; Keynes on, 1–2

Farrer, J. A., applauds empiricism of Smith, 107
Freeport, Sir Andrew: character in *Spectator*, 13, 79; on division of labor, 79; defends trade and traders, 14

Gibbon, Edward, applauds work of Smith, 109
Godwin, William: on avarice, 20; on division of labor and monopoly, 20; on exploitation of worker, 21
Gravity, principle of: association of ideas likened to, 66–67; benevolent feelings likened to, 66, 68–69; and physical order, 66; self-interest likened to, 67 (*see* Paxton, Hutcheson, Bolingbroke, Jenyns); social cohesion likened to, 66

Harris, James: background of, 83–84; on division of labor, 84–86; on basic nature of man, 84; on ultimate state of man, 85; on self-interest and public welfare, 86; on sovereign good, 84; on trade, 85
Hartley, David, likens association of ideas to gravity, 67
Hobbes, Thomas: life of, 29–30; on natural man, 31–32; sees life as motion, 31; on absolute power, 33; on self-interest, 28–29, 34; on the state, 32–34
Hume, David, likens association of ideas to gravity, 66–67
Hutcheson, Francis: background of, 68; likens benevolence to gravity, 69; refutes Hobbes and Mandeville, 68; on moral sense, 68; on self-love, 68–69; and Adam Smith, 68–69
Huxley, Thomas: applauds Smith's principle of sympathy, 107–8; on man as "emotional chameleon," 108

Jenyns, Soame: life of, 71; on chain of being, 71–72; his work criticized, 74–75; on education, 72; his theory of evil, 71–72; attacked by Johnson, 71; and Montesquieu, Mandeville, 73; on pain, 72; on self-interest, 72–74

Johnson, Samuel; approves work of Smith, 109; attacks Jenyns, 71

Kepler, Johann, criticized by Smith, 98–99
Keynes, John Maynard: on classical economics, 1; on influence of "defunct economist," 1; on economists and civilization, 89; on self-interest and public welfare, 1

Labor, division of: and the arts, 85; and civilization, 85, 88; Derham on, 81–82; economic effects of, 77, 79, 111–12; inspires eighteenth-century minds, 77; Freeport on, 79; Harris on, 84–85; answers problem in philosophy, 78–79; and principle of plenitude, 77; Priestley on, 88; social effects of, 77, 79; stultifies worker, 20–21, 123–24
Laissez-faire: Carlyle on, 23; Keynes on, 2–3
Language, Smith attacks misuse of, 99–103
Leibniz, Gotfried Wilhelm, horror of vacancies in nature, 47
Locke, John: and Shaftesbury, 51–53; criticized by Smith, 100
Lovejoy, Arthur: on "Great Chain of Being," 46; on principle of design, 3, 46–48; design shapes educated opinion, 48; on "principle of plenitude," 47; on "unit idea," 3

Maxwell, John: criticizes Cumberland, 82; translator of Cumberland, 39; on social effects of division of labor, 83; on self-interest and public welfare, 83; on social effects of wealth, 82
Moral philosophers, as judges of self-interest, 27

Newton, Sir Isaac: three laws of motion, 66; applauded by Smith, 102

Pascal, Blaise, on continuity of nature, 48
Paxton, Peter: on "pursuit of happiness," 67; likens self-interest to gravity, 67; on self-interest and public welfare, 67
Philosophers of specialization, summary of, 88–89
Philosophy, as uncategorized, unanswered questions, 5
Plato: on pure ideas and the real world, 47 (*see* Lovejoy); Smith on, 99–100